Circuit City believes that simplifying the consumer electronics shopping experience for customers will produce greater loyalty and greater share of wallet while generating attractive returns for shareholders. To provide customers with just what they need, the company will focus on providing product information, to help ease the purchasing process, and offering an array of services, from installations to repairs, to make ownership worry-free. Circuit City is available wherever the customer is — in the store, on the Web, on the phone or in the home. *That* is why customers will say Circuit City provided "Just what I needed" and why they will return for future purchases.

AF675401

MANAGEMENT LETTER

W. Alan McCollough
CHAIRMAN AND CHIEF EXECUTIVE OFFICER

DEAR FELLOW SHAREHOLDERS,

Last year we shared with you some of the steps we planned for fiscal 2005 to move the company toward improved profitability. I am pleased to tell you that fiscal 2005 was a year of progress. We posted growth in total sales, gross profit margin and earnings per share; and we further strengthened our balance sheet. Associates throughout our company accomplished these improvements in a difficult retail environment. Despite the progress, we saw volatility in comparable store sales and customer traffic over the course of the year, and we need to deliver more consistent, positive results in fiscal 2006.

Looking at trends in competition, customer behavior and product innovation, it is clear that operating in the current retail environment will not become any easier. Efforts aimed at improving our profitability are vital, but will not be solely sufficient to achieve the results we seek. We must also focus on innovation to transform our business, and I am excited to tell you that effort is now underway.

Innovation is not new to Circuit City. From CarMax to our new IQ Crew offering, our dedicated Associates have worked together on many projects to create value for our customers and shareholders. With an organization and process to cultivate those ideas, our business can grow in ways we have never before considered. Our strong balance sheet provides the backbone to support these important initiatives in the coming months and years. A great deal of work remains, and new challenges will arise along the way. However, we remain convinced that our best days lie ahead.

Although our financial performance has improved on many metrics, we must continue to work on capitalizing upon our strengths and returning value to you, our shareholders, through a consistent, sustainable financial track record.

FISCAL 2005 ACCOMPLISHMENTS

Let me begin with our accomplishments in fiscal 2005.

International Expansion. The acquisition of the Canadian retailer InterTAN, Inc. was completed in May. Specializing in small stores that carry a broad selection of higher-margin consumer electronic products, the international segment currently operates through more than 900 stores and dealer outlets throughout Canada under the trade names RadioShack®, Rogers Plus® and Battery Plus®. The international segment is a well-run, profitable business that brings with it an experienced sourcing organization and demonstrated ability to develop own-brand products.

Divestiture of the Finance Operation. Also in May, we completed the divestiture of our finance operation by selling the private-label credit card operation to Chase Card Services, formerly Bank One. The sale generated $476 million in net cash proceeds and initiated a strategic relationship with a world-class partner to meet, competitively and creatively, the financing needs of our customers. Circuit City, in conjunction with Chase, introduced a Circuit City Rewards credit card in October. On qualifying purchases at Circuit City, cardholders have the power to choose rewards points or promotional financing. Customers can redeem rewards points for future purchases, enabling Circuit City to show its loyalty to them while encouraging repeat traffic to our stores.

Superstore Openings. Our store revitalization program continued with 31 new stores and 28 relocations of stores to better sites. The results from our relocated stores continue to encourage us, with sales from the relocated stores increasing an average of 25 percent in their first year after grand opening, relative to the rest of the chain. We continue to aggressively seek new store sites to bring our updated shopping experience to both new and loyal customers.

Next-Generation Web Site. In September, we seamlessly launched a next-generation Web site at www.circuitcity.com. The new site features improved navigation; pioneering express pickup of merchandise in all of our stores; and, most importantly, award-winning customer service. We remain pleased with the strong growth in this profitable business.

Brand Re-launch. In October, Circuit City launched a new marketing campaign, centered on the tag line "Just what I needed." The campaign is designed to reinvigorate the Circuit City brand by reminding customers that we offer the full package: the right brands, the right service and unbeatable prices. The launch featured a consistent look, feel and message across all customer touch points.

FINANCIAL PERFORMANCE

Sales and Profits. Total sales increased 6.2 percent to $10.47 billion from $9.86 billion last fiscal year, and comparable store sales increased 0.7 percent. The net earnings from continuing operations were $59.9 million, or 31 cents per share, compared with a net loss from continuing operations of $787,000, or 0 cents per share in fiscal 2004.

FINANCIAL HIGHLIGHTS FROM CONTINUING OPERATIONS

(Dollar amounts in thousands except per share data)	2005	2004	2003
		Years Ended February 28 or 29	
OPERATING RESULTS			
Net sales and operating revenues	**$10,472,364**	$9,857,057	$10,054,864
Earnings (loss) from continuing operations before income taxes	**$ 95,789**	$ (1,240)	$ (5,490)
PER SHARE DATA			
Net earnings (loss) per share from continuing operations:			
Basic	**$ 0.31**	$ —	$ (0.03)
Diluted	**$ 0.31**	$ —	$ (0.03)
Cash dividends paid	**$ 0.07**	$ 0.07	$ 0.07
AT YEAR-END			
Total assets	**$ 3,789,382**	$3,730,526	$ 3,945,456
Common shares outstanding	**188,150,383**	203,899,395	209,954,840
Number of Associates	**45,946**	43,211	38,849

FORWARD-LOOKING STATEMENTS

This report contains forward-looking statements, which are subject to risks and uncertainties. Additional discussion of factors that could cause actual results to differ materially from management's projections, forecasts, estimates and expectations can be found in "Management's Discussion and Analysis of Financial Condition and Results of Operations" contained in this annual report and in the company's Securities and Exchange Commission filings.

Gross Profit Margin. Our gross profit margin improved, benefiting particularly from the inclusion of our international segment. Within the domestic segment, we improved our gross profit margin, and a primary factor was higher sales of extended service plans. We focus on selling complete solutions—i.e. a core product, such as a television, with an extended service plan, home theater system, digital video service through cable or satellite, surge protectors, cables and installation services—because we believe that helps drive sales, margin and customer satisfaction. Additionally, we benefited from lower costs related to the company's product service organization and distribution.

Expenses. Several factors led to increased expenses compared with the prior year including the acquisition of the international segment and increases in advertising expenses to enhance the brand. To offset these increases, we undertook expense-cutting initiatives, including the further refinement of our store operating model and consolidation of field and distribution organizations, as well as the closure of underperforming stores. Due in part to these efforts, we were able to hold domestic store expenses to a slight increase compared with last year while opening 59 new or relocated stores.

Returning Value to You. Finally, in fiscal 2005, we repurchased 19.2 million shares of stock, which in addition to our dividend, enables us to share our cash position with you. Since January 2003, we have repurchased 28.4 million common shares for approximately $344.2 million. In March 2005, we announced that the Board of Directors authorized a $400 million increase in our stock repurchase authorization.

FISCAL 2006 FOCUS

In fiscal 2006, we will continue to drive for improvements in our core business while simultaneously investing in a formal innovation process focused on creating a culture that identifies big ideas and game-changing concepts. I will highlight a few of the largest opportunities.

Improving the Business. Since the transition from a commissioned to an hourly workforce in our stores, we have made substantial improvements in a number of performance measures. We believe, however, there is significant progress yet to make in how we serve our customers. We know that the majority of customers who come into our stores leave without making a purchase. A substantial effort this year will focus on improving that close rate, where even a small improvement can yield big results, as well as ensuring that all customers are provided with the opportunity to find a complete solution to match their needs.

We measure the performance of our stores on a broad range of metrics, and typically we see a fairly wide range of performance across stores on any given measure. Another area of focus this year will be to reduce the size of the performance gap between our best and poorest performing stores. Here, too, even a small improvement in closing the performance gap has the potential to produce substantial improvements in operating results.

Philip J. Schoonover
PRESIDENT

Michael E. Foss
EXECUTIVE VICE PRESIDENT
CHIEF FINANCIAL OFFICER

Eric A. Jonas, Jr.
SENIOR VICE PRESIDENT
HUMAN RESOURCES

Brian E. Levy
PRESIDENT AND CHIEF EXECUTIVE OFFICER, INTERTAN

In fiscal 2005, we made progress in working capital management in terms of net-owned inventory and believe opportunity for significant further progress remains. During fiscal 2006, we would expect to improve our forecasting accuracy, providing for smoother product transitions with less obsolete product, and to further reduce our net owned inventory.

One identified opportunity for improvement in fiscal 2005 was driving consistent customer traffic. This year, we will invest in systems that can provide a more robust measure of the effectiveness of our promotions. We will use feedback to create more effective advertising, which will drive traffic and sales and also should improve our brand image with consumers.

Innovation. We are creating an innovation engine. Innovation teams will generate many ideas, then pursue, develop and test concepts aimed at the creation of real value and the transformation of our business for the future. Expect to see us try many new things, some of which will likely fail, but all of which will result in learning. We will take calculated risks and make fact-based decisions, ultimately adopting winning ideas. Opportunities identified and captured by this innovation process should contribute to a sustainable long-term growth rate, and in return, generate growth in shareholder value.

To begin the process, we have identified a manageable number of initiatives to pursue in fiscal 2006, and I will share a few examples.

- Our heritage is in television, and we continue to believe that the living room will serve as the hub for family entertainment. The objective of one innovation team will center on Circuit City becoming *the* retail destination for home entertainment products and services.
- Consumer electronics products continue to evolve with more features and functionality at lower prices—a boon to consumers who can figure out how to make the functionality work for them in their everyday lives. To provide our customers with just what they need, a second innovation team will focus on the development of a breakthrough consumer electronics services business that will offer an array of services, from installations to repairs, to provide a single point of contact for the customers and make the ownership period worry-free.
- Finally, because more of our customers seek information and products in places other than our stores, a third team will work to capture multi-channel sales opportunities more than ever before. Circuit City will be there, whether in the store, on the Web, on the phone or in the home, to put the solution together for the consumer. *That* is why our customers will say Circuit City provided "Just what I needed" and why they will return to us for future purchases.

LEADERSHIP CHANGES

We are delighted to have significantly strengthened our management team. We now benefit from adding new talent as well as shifting proven Circuit City veterans into different roles.

Most notably, we welcome the addition of consumer electronics industry veteran Phil Schoonover as President. Phil gained experience in various roles at Tweeter, Tops Appliance City, Sony and, most recently, Best Buy. Phil has a strong background in developing new ideas and bringing them to the marketplace. At Best Buy, he was an integral player in a number of key initiatives, including customer centricity. I believe that Phil is a great addition to our leadership team, and I am confident that he will play a key role in the progress towards building a new Circuit City.

In February, we announced the promotion of Mike Foss to executive vice president as he continues his role as chief financial officer. During his tenure, Mike has brought extensive financial expertise and made significant contributions to the company through his commitment to operations improvement.

We were also pleased to promote Eric Jonas to lead our efforts in human resources, where we continually strive to both recruit new talent and serve our current Associates with attractive and relevant compensation and benefits.

When we acquired InterTAN in May, we also brought on board their strong management team led by Brian Levy. Brian, who now heads our international segment, has extensive experience operating small store formats.

Be assured that our associates are committed to and focused on driving shareholder value by continually improving their execution and working tirelessly to deliver more profitable results. We will not rest as we continue to build a new Circuit City.

W. ALAN MCCOLLOUGH
Chairman and Chief Executive Officer
Circuit City Stores, Inc.
April 11, 2005

UNITED STATES
SECURITIES AND EXCHANGE COMMISSION
WASHINGTON, D.C. 20549

FORM 10-K

[X] ANNUAL REPORT PURSUANT TO SECTION 13 OR 15(d) OF THE SECURITIES EXCHANGE ACT OF 1934

For the fiscal year ended February 28, 2005

OR

[ ] TRANSITION REPORT PURSUANT TO SECTION 13 OR 15(d) OF THE SECURITIES EXCHANGE ACT OF 1934

For the transition period from_________ to _________

Commission File No.: 1-5767

CIRCUIT CITY STORES, INC.

(Exact name of registrant as specified in its charter)

VIRGINIA (State or other jurisdiction of incorporation or organization)	**54-0493875** (I.R.S. Employer Identification No.)
9950 Mayland Drive **Richmond, Virginia** (Address of principal executive offices)	**23233** (Zip Code)

Registrant's telephone number, including area code: **(804) 527-4000**

Securities registered pursuant to Section 12(b) of the Act:

Title of each class	**Name of each exchange on which registered**
Common Stock, Par Value $0.50 per share	New York Stock Exchange
Rights to Purchase Preferred Stock, Series E, Par Value $20.00 per share	New York Stock Exchange

Securities registered pursuant to Section 12(g) of the Act: None

Indicate by check mark whether the registrant (1) has filed all reports required to be filed by Section 13 or 15(d) of the Securities Exchange Act of 1934 during the preceding 12 months (or for such shorter period that the registrant was required to file such reports), and (2) has been subject to such filing requirements for the past 90 days. Yes ✓ No ___

Indicate by check mark if disclosure of delinquent filers pursuant to Item 405 of Regulation S-K (§229.405 of this chapter) is not contained herein, and will not be contained, to the best of registrant's knowledge, in definitive proxy or information statements incorporated by reference in Part III of this Form 10-K or any amendment to this Form 10-K [ ].

Indicate by check mark whether the registrant is an accelerated filer (as defined in Rule 12b-2 of the Act). Yes ✓ No ___

The aggregate market value of the registrant's common shares held by non-affiliates as of August 31, 2004, which was the last business day of the registrant's most recently completed second fiscal quarter, was $2,531,528,283 based upon the closing price of these shares as reported by the New York Stock Exchange on that date.

On March 31, 2005, the company had outstanding 188,274,230 shares of common stock.

DOCUMENTS INCORPORATED BY REFERENCE

Portions of the company's Definitive Proxy Statement dated May 13, 2005, furnished to shareholders of the company in connection with the 2005 Annual Meeting of Shareholders are incorporated by reference in Part III of this Annual Report on Form 10-K.

TABLE OF CONTENTS

PART I

Item 1. Business.

Circuit City Stores, Inc. is a leading specialty retailer of consumer electronics, home office products, entertainment software and related services. Circuit City was incorporated under the laws of the Commonwealth of Virginia in 1949. Its corporate headquarters are located at 9950 Mayland Drive, Richmond, Virginia. The company has two reportable segments: its domestic segment and its international segment. For fiscal 2005, net sales and operating revenues were $10.02 billion for the domestic segment and $454.9 million for the international segment. Prior to the second quarter of fiscal 2005, we had a third reportable segment our finance operation.

The domestic segment is primarily engaged in the business of selling brand-name consumer electronics, personal computers, entertainment software and services in Circuit City Superstores and mall-based stores in the United States and via the Web at www.circuitcity.com. At February 28, 2005, the company's domestic segment operated 612 Superstores and 5 mall-based stores in 158 U.S. media markets.

The international segment, which is comprised of the operations of InterTAN, Inc., is primarily engaged in the business of selling private-label and brand-name consumer electronics products in Canada. At February 28, 2005, the international segment conducted business through 966 retail stores and dealer outlets, which consisted of 521 stores operating under the trade name RadioShack®, 331 dealer outlets, 88 Rogers Plus® stores and 26 Battery Plus® stores. In addition to the 966 retail stores and dealer outlets, the international segment conducts business through 64 wholesale relationships.

InterTAN s stores operating under the trade name RadioShack typically incorporate a small store format and are strategically located in malls and shopping centers; each store provides the customer with convenience and readily available products and services to meet a wide range of consumer electronic needs, including digital technologies and unique electronic gadgets. Dealer outlets are independent retail businesses that operate under their own trade names but are permitted, under dealer agreements, to purchase any of the products sold by company-operated stores. The dealer agreements contain a sub-license permitting dealers to designate its consumer electronics department or business as a RadioShack Dealer. Rogers Plus stores are operated by the company and are dedicated primarily to the sale of wireless services, including related hardware, offered by Rogers Wireless, Inc. Battery Plus stores are operated by the company and sell batteries and other specialty consumer electronics products. The use of the term "company-operated stores" refers to our stores operating under the RadioShack, Rogers Plus and Battery Plus names.

All stores currently operating under license from RadioShack Corporation will be re-branded as "THE SOURCE BY CIRCUIT CITY" on or before June 30, 2005. See additional discussion in Item 3, Legal Proceedings, of this Annual Report on Form 10-K.

Additional discussion of Circuit City's operating segments is included in Item 7, Management's Discussion and Analysis of Financial Condition and Results of Operations, and in Note 18, Segment Information, of the Notes to Consolidated Financial Statements, included in Item 8, Financial Statements and Supplementary Data, of this Annual Report on Form 10-K.

The company's plan is to improve its core business and introduce a disciplined innovation process that will enable future growth. Stabilizing sales and driving improvements in profitability and working capital management are important steps in turning around the business. Circuit City must seek ways to expand its reach beyond loyal customers by finding new customers, providing new offerings and continually searching for new opportunities. To do this, the company has formalized an innovation organization and process to cultivate new ideas that will grow its business in ways it never before considered and create value for its customers and shareholders.

Acquisition of InterTAN, Inc.

In May 2004, Circuit City completed its acquisition of InterTAN, Inc. for cash consideration of $259.3 million, which includes transaction costs and is net of cash acquired of $30.6 million. In addition to giving Circuit City a greater product-sourcing capability and the ability to accelerate the offering of private-label merchandise to its customers, the acquisition of InterTAN gives Circuit City its first presence in the Canadian market. For information regarding the company's risk associated with our international segment, see Forward-Looking Statements included in Item 7, Management's Discussion and Analysis of Financial Condition and Results of Operations, and Translation of Financial Results included in Item 7A, Quantitative and Qualitative Disclosures about Market Risk, of this Annual Report of Form 10-K.

Sale of Finance Operations

In May 2004, the company completed the sale of its private-label finance operation, comprised of its private-label and co-branded Visa credit card programs, to Chase Card Services, formerly Bank One Corporation. Results from the private-label finance operation are included in finance income on the consolidated statements of operations. The company entered into a Consumer Credit Card Program Agreement under which Chase Card Services is offering private-label and co-branded credit cards to new and existing customers. The company is compensated under the arrangement primarily based on the number of new accounts opened less promotional financing costs that exceed a negotiated base amount. The earnings contribution from the Chase credit card program is included in net sales and operating revenues on the consolidated statement of operations.

In November 2003, the company completed the sale of its bankcard finance operation, which included Visa and MasterCard credit card receivables and related cash reserves, to FleetBoston Financial. Results from the bankcard finance operation are presented as results from discontinued operations on the consolidated statements of operations. The sale agreement included a transition services agreement under which employees of the company's finance operation continued to service the bankcard accounts until final conversion of the bankcard portfolio to FleetBoston, which occurred in April 2004. Through that date, FleetBoston reimbursed the company for operating costs incurred during the transition period. The company incurred severance costs ratably through the final conversion date.

Operations

Circuit City has a highly integrated business model, which allows customers to shop across numerous channels.

Domestic segment store operations are overseen by the president of our domestic retail stores. Domestic retail operations are divided into 10 regions, which are under the supervision of regional vice presidents. The 10 regions are comprised of 63 districts, which are overseen by district managers who regularly visit stores to monitor store operations and meet with store directors.

Domestic segment Superstores are typically staffed with 40 to 80 full-time and part-time Associates including

- sales support personnel, such as customer service Associates, product specialists and stockpersons;
- two or more sales managers;
- an operations manager; and
- a store director.

At February 28, 2005, the domestic segment had 42,425 hourly and salaried employees. None of these employees is subject to a collective bargaining agreement. The company may employ additional personnel during peak selling seasons. In fiscal 2004, the company outsourced the applicant screening process and reduced the time to hire a new store Associate by more than 50 percent and thus significantly decreased the time required to complete seasonal hiring. The company has a single hourly pay structure for the domestic segment's non-management sales force.

International segment company-operated stores are divided into five regions, which are overseen by regional directors. The five regions are further divided into 28 districts, which are under the supervision of district managers who regularly visit stores to monitor store operations. Dealer outlets are divided into seven areas across Canada, each of which is under the supervision of an area sales manager.

International segment company-operated stores are typically staffed by 2 to 15 Associates, including full-time and part-time commissioned sales Associates and a store manager. At February 28, 2005, the international segment had 3,521 hourly and salaried employees. Approximately 109 of these employees, who are engaged in warehousing and distribution operations, are represented by a union. In April 2003, the terms of a three-year collective bargaining agreement were ratified with these employees. The company considers its relationship with these employees to be good.

Associates in our domestic and international segments receive frequent training and development through interactive e-learning courses, training workbooks and management-driven in-store mentoring. Training includes developing selling skills, product knowledge with an emphasis on new technology, customer service and store operations. Associates use Circuit City's Web site as an additional training resource for product knowledge. Management training programs are designed to prepare the company's leaders and include Web-based training, in-store activities and classroom instruction.

Merchandising

The company offers a broad selection of products and services through its stores, on the Web and via telephone. The major merchandise product categories are

- **video,** including televisions, imaging products, DVD hardware, camcorders, digital cameras, digital video services, furniture and related accessories;
- **information technology,** including personal computer hardware, telecommunications products, PDAs and related product accessories;
- **audio,** including home audio products, mobile audio products, portable audio products and related accessories; and
- **entertainment software,** including movie software, music software, game software, game hardware and personal computer software.

Services are another important part of the company's offering to consumers. Examples of the provided services include narrowband, broadband, wireless telephone, voice-over IP, digital video services, extended warranty programs, satellite radio, computer upgrades and repairs, car audio installation and in-home video installation.

The company's direct-to-consumer business has grown rapidly since the launch of its Web site in 1999. Through Circuit City Direct, which serves customers via circuitcity.com and 1-800-THE-CITY, customers have access to a wide selection of consumer electronics, technology and entertainment products and related services as well as around-the-clock customer service. Circuitcity.com offers more than 125,000 customer ratings and reviews of products, as well as in-depth product and technology information. The company re-launched its award-winning Web site in September 2004. The next-generation site offers improved navigation, ease of use and better merchandising. Customers may view real-time in-store inventory of products selected on circuitcity.com, purchase the products online, and pick up the products in a nearby store typically within one hour from the time of purchase.

To ensure consistency, each domestic store follows centrally-controlled, detailed operating procedures and merchandising programs, including procedures for inventory maintenance and merchandise displays. Merchandise pricing may vary by market to reflect local competitive conditions.

The international segment's strategy focuses on a merchandise offering designed to grow both sales and gross profit margin. Fundamental to this plan is

- a product offering that includes private-label and name-brand products;
- an emphasis on strategically selected high margin core categories for which the company has a strong position in its markets; and
- management of the percentage of lower gross profit margin products to the overall sales mix.

Supply Chain

Circuit City relies on a best sourcing strategy. Depending on the type of product, the company procures merchandise from a variety of sources and methods, including new and existing vendors, reverse auctions and direct relationships with manufacturers. The company also utilizes its global sourcing capability gained through the acquisition of InterTAN. The company's goal is to find the lowest priced products with the highest quality for customers.

As a retailer primarily of branded consumer electronics that relies upon its ability to offer consumers a comprehensive and attractive assortment of merchandise and services, Circuit City depends upon strong and stable supplier relationships. During fiscal 2005, the domestic segment's five largest suppliers accounted for approximately 48 percent of merchandise purchased. The major suppliers included Sony, Hewlett Packard, Panasonic, Samsung and Toshiba. The international segment's five largest suppliers accounted for approximately 38 percent of its merchandise purchased and included Motorola, Rogers Wireless, Panasonic, Acer America Corporation and Hewlett-Packard.

The loss or disruption in supply from any one of these major suppliers could have a material adverse effect on our revenue and earnings. We have no indication that any of our suppliers will discontinue selling us merchandise. We have not experienced significant difficulty in maintaining satisfactory sources of supply, and we generally expect that adequate sources of supply will continue to exist for the types of merchandise sold in our stores.

Circuit City offers an increasing amount of own-branded merchandise to complement its branded strategy. These unique brands, including Nexxtech, Centrios, Wasaki, Sector 7, esa, Liquid Video, Verge and Anika, supplement one of the best selections of name-brand products in the consumer electronics industry and provide an even broader selection to customers. Through Circuit City Global Sourcing, Ltd., a wholly owned subsidiary, the company has developed internal sourcing capabilities including sourcing offices in China, Hong Kong and Taiwan. This effort has resulted in the introduction of more than 3,000 new products, which are sold through the company's stores, Web site and via the telephone.

The domestic segment has made improvements to its supply chain, including

- more closely matching the timing of merchandise receipt into distribution centers and deployment to stores with expected sales levels;
- selectively adjusting merchandise display quantities; and
- consolidating its distribution organization to reduce costs.

During fiscal 2006, the company will focus on improving in-stock positions, reducing levels of net-owned inventory, increasing inventory turnover, decreasing markdowns and enhancing product offering. During fiscal 2006, the company also will work to optimize the product assortment and to generate a greater impact on traffic, profit and brand image from advertising and promotions.

Distribution

As of February 28, 2005, the domestic segment operated

- six automated regional electronics distribution centers;

- one smaller automated distribution center that primarily handles larger non-conveyable products, such as big screen televisions;
- one automated centralized entertainment software distribution center that serves all stores; and
- one import consolidation center.

Most products are shipped from manufacturers directly to the distribution centers. Circuit City believes that the use of distribution centers enables it to efficiently distribute a broad selection of merchandise to its stores, reduce inventory levels at individual stores, benefit from volume purchasing and maintain inventory control. Some entertainment software is received directly from the manufacturer by the stores in order to reduce costs and ensure that new release titles are promptly available to customers.

The international segment's stores are replenished primarily through one distribution center in Barrie, Ontario, Canada.

Domestic Store Revitalization

During fiscal 2001, Circuit City introduced a new Superstore format that features increased selling square footage, a brighter, more contemporary look and an open, easily navigable floor plan conducive to browsing. The format allows the company to put all products, except those that are too large for customers to carry themselves, on the sales floor. The company also has improved product adjacencies so that customers can conveniently shop for products and accessories related to their core product purchase. Shopping carts, baskets and centralized cash register checkouts add to the convenience of the increased number of "take-with" products in the stores.

During fiscal 2005, continuing the effort to update the store base to this new format, the company opened 31 incremental Superstores, relocated 28 Superstores and fully remodeled one Superstore. The following table summarizes the progress of the domestic store revitalization program over the last five fiscal years.

Fiscal	Store Openings	Store Relocations	Full Remodels	Store Closures	Superstores at End of Fiscal Year
2005	31	28	1	19	612
2004	8	18	4	20[(a)]	599
2003	8[(b)]	11	3	1	611
2002	11	8	12	1	604
2001	24[(c)]	1	26[(d)]	1	594
Total	82	66	46	42	

(a) On February 29, 2004, the company closed one store in advance of opening a replacement store in the first quarter of fiscal 2005. The replacement store is included in fiscal 2005 store relocations.

(b) One of the stores opened in fiscal 2003 was closed in February 2005.

(c) Two of the 24 new store openings did not have the new format.

(d) Two of the locations that were fully remodeled in fiscal 2001 were closed in February 2004.

From the beginning of fiscal 2001 through February 28, 2005, a total of 189 Superstores, or 31 percent of the company's 612 domestic Superstores, had been newly constructed under the new format, relocated or fully remodeled. During fiscal 2006, the company expects to open 30 to 40 domestic stores, of which it expects approximately half will be relocations.

Information Systems

The domestic segment's in-store point-of-sale (POS) system maintains an online record of all transactions and allows management to track performance by region, store and store Associate. The information gathered by the system supports automatic replenishment of in-store inventory from the regional distribution centers and is incorporated into product buying decisions. The in-store POS system is seamlessly integrated with the company's e-commerce Web site. This integration provides the capability for in-store pickup of merchandise ordered from the Internet and allows for in-store ordering of merchandise for shipment directly to the customer's home.

For our international segment, each of the company-operated stores has one or more computers that serve as POS terminals and are linked to the operational headquarters. This information network provides detailed sales and margin information on a daily basis, updates the customer database and acts as a monitor of individual store performance. The POS systems also are linked directly to a system used to automatically replenish a store's stock as inventory is sold.

The company's information systems strategy is to use solutions available in the marketplace instead of developing software in-house, allowing Circuit City to utilize its resources to enhance profitability and to create a competitive advantage. As part of an effort to eliminate complex, custom-developed information systems, the domestic segment plans to roll out a new POS system during fiscal 2006. The company expects the in-store system to be coupled with new data warehousing capabilities that will improve internal processes, streamline applications and allow more timely analysis of data. In fiscal 2006, the domestic segment also expects to invest in systems that enhance the analysis of the effectiveness of its advertising.

Marketing

During the third quarter of fiscal 2005, Circuit City's domestic segment introduced a marketing campaign designed to have one consistent message that would resonate with consumers. The same message can be seen or heard in print, on television, through direct marketing, on the Web, on the radio and in stores. The brand image, based on the tagline "Just what I needed," embodies what Circuit City offers consumers: a complete solution with the right products and services, the ability to shop the way they want to shop, unbeatable prices and knowledgeable product specialists. The domestic segment concurrently introduced a marketing campaign specifically directed to the Hispanic community with the same focused message. In order to optimize the effectiveness of its marketing efforts, the domestic segment aligns its level of marketing spending and the mix of advertising vehicles used with the size and type of market, competition and cost factors.

Also during fiscal 2005, the domestic segment introduced a rewards credit card in partnership with Chase Card Services. Cardholders have the power to choose rewards points or promotional financing for qualifying purchases at Circuit City. The points can be redeemed for future purchases, enabling Circuit City to reward its loyal customers while encouraging repeat traffic to its stores.

The international segment is among the largest retail advertisers in Canada. The company advertises through multiple channels including newspaper, television, an annual catalog, direct mailings and radio.

Competition

The consumer electronics retail industry is highly competitive. Competitors include other consumer electronics retailers, discount retailers, warehouse clubs, home office retailers, Internet-based retailers and direct-to-consumer alternatives. Discount retailers continue to increase consumer electronics offerings, particularly on entry-level and less complex products.

Circuit City's domestic segment differentiates itself from competitors by offering outstanding customer service; offering competitive prices; providing complete product and service assortments; and providing consumers the option of multi-channel shopping.

The international segment differentiates itself from other consumer electronics retailers in Canada through its range of products and its service orientation. InterTAN has established a market position in important growth categories, including wireless and other digital products, as well as in unique electronic gadgets.

Intellectual Property

The company's principal trademarks and service marks, which are "Circuit City," "Circuit City Direct," "Circuit City Express," "InterTAN" and "Just what I needed," either have been registered, or have trademark applications pending, with the United States Patent and Trademark Office and with the trademark registries of various foreign jurisdictions. The company also owns various patents and trademarks related to consumer electronic goods designed and manufactured by third parties for Circuit City. The company's rights in these trademarks and services continue for as long as they are used. The Company believes that the "Circuit City" name and the circle logo design have significant value and are important to its business.

The company's InterTAN subsidiary currently licenses marks from RadioShack Corporation to operate retail consumer electronics outlets under the RadioShack® name in Canada. That licensing agreement is the subject of litigation. Additional discussion of the litigation is included in Item 3, Legal Proceedings, of this Annual Report on Form 10-K. The company has trademark applications pending in both the United States and Canada for "THE SOURCE BY CIRCUIT CITY." All stores currently operating under license from RadioShack Corporation will be re-branded on or before June 30, 2005. The international segment also operates stores under the registered trademarks Rogers Plus and Battery Plus.

Seasonality

Like many retailers, Circuit City's revenues are typically greatest during the fourth fiscal quarter because it includes the majority of the holiday selling season. A corresponding pre-season inventory build-up during the third fiscal quarter is typically associated with this higher sales period.

Working Capital

The company funds capital expenditures and working capital needs through available cash, borrowing capacity under its $500 million credit facility, landlord reimbursements and sale-leaseback transactions. Additional discussion of Circuit City's Liquidity and Capital Resources is included in Item 7, Management's Discussion and Analysis of Financial Condition and Results of Operations, of this Annual Report on Form 10-K.

Capital Structure

From February 7, 1997, to October 1, 2002, the common stock of Circuit City Stores, Inc. consisted of two common stock series that were intended to reflect the performance of the company's two businesses during that period. The Circuit City Group common stock was intended to reflect the performance of the Circuit City consumer electronics stores and related operations, as well as the shares of CarMax Group common stock reserved for the Circuit City Group or for issuance to holders of Circuit City Group common stock. The CarMax Group common stock was intended to reflect the performance of the CarMax auto superstores and related operations.

Effective October 1, 2002, the CarMax auto superstore business was separated from the Circuit City consumer electronics business through a tax-free transaction in which CarMax, Inc., formerly a wholly owned subsidiary of Circuit City Stores, Inc., became an independent, separately traded public company. Following the separation, the Circuit City Group common stock was renamed Circuit City common stock. CarMax results are presented as results from discontinued operations on the consolidated statements of operations. The company recorded no gain or loss as a result of the separation. Additional discussion of the separation is included in Note 17(B), Discontinued Operations, of the Notes to Consolidated Financial Statements, included in Item 8, Financial Statements and Supplementary Data, of this Annual Report on Form 10-K.

Discontinued Divx Operation

Through Digital Video Express, 75 percent of which was owned by the company, Circuit City developed a new digital video system for watching movies at home. Divx was primarily engaged in the business of licensing this technology and replicating and distributing specially encrypted DVDs at wholesale. Circuit City was allocated 100 percent of Divx's losses from Divx's inception. In fiscal 2000, Digital Video Express announced that it would cease marketing the Divx home video system and discontinue operations. Divx results are presented as results from discontinued operations on the consolidated statements of operations. Additional discussion of the discontinued Divx operation is included in Note 17(C), Discontinued Operations, of the Notes to Consolidated Financial Statements, included in Item 8, Financial Statements and Supplementary Data, of this Annual Report on Form 10-K.

Appliance Exit

In the second quarter of fiscal 2001, the company began to exit the major appliance category. This process was completed in November 2000. To exit the appliance business, the company closed eight distribution centers and eight service centers. The company subleases the majority of these leased properties.

Available Information

Circuit City makes available, free of charge on its Web site, its Annual Report on Form 10-K, quarterly reports on Form 10-Q, current reports on Form 8-K and any amendments to those reports as soon as practicable after electronically filing the material with or furnishing the material to the Securities and Exchange Commission. These documents may be viewed by visiting the company's investor information Web site at http://investor.circuitcity.com and selecting the "SEC Filings" link under the "Investor Info" header.

The company also makes available, free of charge on its Web site, the charters of the Audit Committee, Nominating and Governance Committee and Compensation and Personnel Committee as well as the code of conduct and the board practices and policies adopted by the board of directors. These documents may be viewed by visiting the investor information Web site at http://investor.circuitcity.com and selecting the "Corporate Governance" link under the "Company Info" header.

References to the company's Web site do not constitute incorporation by reference of the information contained on the Web site, and the information contained on the Web site is not part of this document.

Item 2. Properties.

The following table summarizes the geographic location of our retail stores at February 28, 2005.

	Domestic Segment		
	Superstores	Mall-based Stores	Total
Alabama	8	-	8
Arizona	12	-	12
Arkansas	3	-	3
California	85	-	85
Colorado	12	-	12
Connecticut	8	-	8
Delaware	2	-	2
Florida	46	-	46
Georgia	21	1	22
Hawaii	1	-	1
Idaho	2	-	2
Illinois	31	-	31
Indiana	13	-	13
Kansas	3	-	3
Kentucky	7	-	7
Louisiana	10	-	10
Maine	2	-	2
Maryland	17	-	17
Massachusetts	16	1	17
Michigan	21	-	21
Minnesota	8	1	9
Mississippi	4	-	4
Missouri	11	-	11
Nebraska	1	-	1
Nevada	5	-	5
New Hampshire	5	-	5
New Jersey	17	-	17
New Mexico	2	-	2
New York	32	-	32
North Carolina	19	1	20
Ohio	25	-	25
Oklahoma	5	-	5
Oregon	7	-	7
Pennsylvania	28	-	28
Rhode Island	1	-	1
South Carolina	8	-	8
Tennessee	12	-	12
Texas	49	-	49
Utah	5	-	5
Vermont	1	-	1
Virginia	24	1	25
Washington	11	-	11
West Virginia	4	-	4
Wisconsin	7	-	7
Wyoming	1	-	1
	612	5	617

	International Segment				
	Radio Shack	Dealer Outlets	Rogers Plus	Battery Plus	Total
Alberta	48	54	14	4	120
British Columbia	61	47	6	–	114
Manitoba	13	19	4	–	36
New Brunswick	15	13	1	–	29
Newfoundland	7	13	–	–	20
North West Territories	1	3	–	–	4
Novia Scotia	20	12	2	–	34
Nunavut	–	1	–	–	1
Ontario	219	94	35	20	368
Prince Edward Island	3	5	1	–	9
Quebec	118	51	23	2	194
Saskatchewan	15	18	2	–	35
Yukon	1	1	–	–	2
	521	331	88	26	966

The following table summarizes the lease expiration dates of our domestic segment at February 28, 2005.

Fiscal Year of Lease Expiration	Stores
2006 through 2010	87
2011 through 2015	84
2016 through 2020	362
2021 through 2025	78
	611
Company-owned stores	6
Total stores at February 28, 2005	617

Of the domestic segment's stores open at February 28, 2005, the company owns six stores and leases the remaining 611 stores. All nine of the domestic segment's distribution centers are leased. The company owns one of its five domestic segment's service centers. For its corporate headquarters, the company owns most of the land, but leases two buildings. The company leases space for all warehouse, service and office facilities except as otherwise noted.

Circuit City's international segment owns a 402,000 square-foot building containing office and warehouse space and a retail location in Barrie, Ontario, Canada, where the headquarters of the international segment are located. With the exception of a retail store located on this property, the international segment's operations are conducted in leased facilities. The dealer outlets included in the preceding table are independent retail businesses that operate under their own trade names but are permitted, under dealer agreements, to purchase any of the products sold by InterTAN. In addition to the 966 stores and dealer outlets, the international segment conducts business through 64 wholesale relationships.

For information regarding the company's lease obligations, see Note 12, Lease Commitments, of the Notes to Consolidated Financial Statements, included in Item 8, Financial Statement and Supplementary Data, of this Annual Report on Form 10-K.

Item 3. Legal Proceedings.

On March 31, 2004, Circuit City announced a public tender offer to purchase the stock of InterTAN. Circuit City completed the acquisition and InterTAN became a wholly owned subsidiary of Circuit City on May 19, 2004. Among other things, InterTAN operates retail consumer electronics outlets under the RadioShack® name in Canada under a licensing agreement with a subsidiary of RadioShack Corporation. InterTAN also operates under two other agreements with RadioShack and its subsidiaries ("RadioShack"): a merchandising agreement and an advertising agreement.

After the March 31, 2004 announcement, RadioShack asserted early termination of all three agreements under a variety of theories and on a variety of proposed termination dates. RadioShack asserts that InterTAN failed to pay an annual fee in material breach of the advertising agreement and, alternatively, that a "without cause" termination of the advertising agreement triggers termination of the other agreements.

On April 5, 2004, RadioShack filed suit against InterTAN in Tarrant County, Texas, and amended that suit on April 27, 2004 (the "RadioShack litigation"). InterTAN disputes the various termination scenarios alleged by RadioShack and is vigorously defending against those claims. InterTAN also has filed claims for disparagement and unfair business practices against RadioShack. The parties argued a RadioShack motion for partial summary judgment on February 3, 2005. On March 24, 2005 the court issued an order on that motion stating that the three agreements were terminated no later than December 31, 2004. If that ruling stands, there would be a six-month wind down period under the license agreement until June 30, 2005.

Circuit City continues to believe that RadioShack is not entitled to early termination of the agreements and that InterTAN has substantial defenses to the RadioShack claims. Circuit City and InterTAN intend to vigorously defend the claims and exercise InterTAN's rights under the agreements, as well as any appeal rights.

Because of the ongoing legal conflict with RadioShack, Circuit City has been taking steps to position its Canadian operations for continued success, regardless of the outcome of this litigation. Circuit City believes that this litigation will not have a material adverse effect on the company's financial condition or results of operations.

Item 4. Submission of Matters to a Vote of Security Holders.

No matter was submitted to a vote of security holders during the fourth quarter of the fiscal year ended February 28, 2005.

Executive Officers of the Company

The company is not aware of any family relationship between any executive officers of the company or any executive officer and any director of the company. The executive officers are generally elected annually and serve for one year or until their successors are elected. The next general election of officers is expected to occur in June 2005. The following table identifies the executive officers of the company at April 30, 2005.

Name	Age	Office
W. Alan McCollough	55	Chairman Chief Executive Officer
Philip J. Schoonover	45	President
Michael E. Foss	47	Executive Vice President Chief Financial Officer
Brian E. Levy	46	President and Chief Executive Officer, InterTAN
George D. Clark, Jr.	45	Senior Vice President President, Circuit City - Retail Stores
Ronald G. Cuthbertson	48	Senior Vice President Supply Chain and Inventory Management
William C. Denney	48	Senior Vice President General Merchandise Manager

Fiona P. Dias	39	Senior Vice President President Circuit City Direct
Philip J. Dunn	52	Senior Vice President Treasurer and Controller
Eric A. Jonas, Jr.	50	Senior Vice President Human Resources
Michael L. Jones	49	Senior Vice President Chief Information Officer
Gary M. Mierenfeld	53	Senior Vice President Store Development, Procurement, Distribution and Service
Douglas T. Moore	48	Senior Vice President Chief Merchandising Officer
Marc J. Sieger	36	Senior Vice President General Merchandise Manager
Ernest V. Speranza	59	Senior Vice President Chief Marketing Officer
Randall W. Wick	44	Senior Vice President General Merchandise Manager

Mr. McCollough is chairman of the board and chief executive officer and a member of the board's executive committee. He joined the company in 1987 as general manager of corporate operations. He was elected assistant vice president in 1989, vice president and Central Division president in 1991, senior vice president - merchandising in 1994, president and chief operating officer in 1997, chief executive officer in June 2000 and chairman of the board in June 2002.

Mr. Schoonover joined the company in October 2004 as executive vice president and chief merchandising officer. He was elected president in February 2005. Before joining the company, he was executive vice president – customer segments at Best Buy Co., Inc., a retailer of consumer electronics, home-office products, entertainment software, appliances and related services, from April 2004 until September 2004. He joined Best Buy in 1995 and previously served as executive vice president – new business development from February 2002 until April 2004; executive vice president – digital technology solutions from February 200[illegible] until February 2002; and senior vice president – merchandising for five years. Before joining Best Buy, Mr. Schoonover was an executive vice president at TOPS Appliance City, a retailer of home appliances and consumer electronics, and held senior marketing positions with Sony Corporation of America, a global entertainment company.

Mr. Foss joined the company in 2003 as senior vice president and chief financial officer. He was promoted to executive vice president in 2005. Before joining the company, he was executive vice president of corporate/business development for TeleTech Holdings Inc., a global provider of customer management solutions for large companies, from 2001 to 2003; president of TeleTech Companies Group, an operating division of TeleTech Holdings, Inc., from 2000 to 2001; and executive vice president and chief financial officer of TeleTech Holdings and president of TeleTech Companies Group from 1999 to 2000. Mr. Foss was employed by Eastman Kodak Corporation, a company engaged in developing, manufacturing and marketing traditional and digital imaging products, services and solutions, from 1997 to 1999 in various senior positions, including chief executive officer of Kodak's Picturevision Inc. subsidiary.

Mr. Levy joined InterTAN in 1998 as president and chief operating officer. He was named president and chief executive officer of InterTAN in 1999 and became a Circuit City officer in 2004 upon Circuit City's acquisition of InterTAN. Before joining InterTAN, Mr. Levy was employed for more than 20 years with Tandy Corporation, then the parent of RadioShack Corporation, serving in various positions including senior vice president in the RadioShack division.

Mr. Clark joined the company in 1983. He was promoted to store manager in 1987, district manager in 1992 and regional vice president in 1993. He was named assistant vice president in 1995, vice president and Central Division president in 1997, Eastern Division president in 2002, senior vice president in 2003, and general merchandise manager for Technology in September 2004. He was named president, Circuit City - Retail Stores in March 2005.

Mr. Cuthbertson joined the company in March 2005 as senior vice president, supply chain and inventory management. Before joining the company, he was president and chief executive officer of Southport Consulting, Inc., a management consulting company. Prior to his role at Southport Consulting, he was employed at Best Buy Co., Inc. from 1999 to 2004 and served in numerous roles including enterprise vice president, with concurrent roles of vice president Best Buy International and vice president global sourcing, and executive vice president, merchandising, marketing and supply chain at Best Buy Canada Ltd. Mr. Cuthbertson also served in various positions at Sears Canada Inc., a division of Sears, Roebuck & Co., a retailer of home merchandise, apparel and automotive products and related services, from 1979 to 1998.

Mr. Denney joined the company in 1979. After serving as store manager in numerous locations, he moved into a regional merchandising role. Mr. Denney served as divisional merchandising manager for the southern division from 1986 to 1994. He was named corporate director of advertising and marketing in 1994, assistant vice president in 1995, vice president - general merchandise manager in 2002 and senior vice president in 2003. Mr. Denney is the general merchandise manager for Entertainment, Mobile and Portable Audio.

Ms. Dias joined the company in 2000 as senior vice president – marketing. She was named president of Circuit City Direct in 2003. Before joining the company, she was chief marketing officer at Stick Networks, Inc., a wireless software company, during 2000; vice president – marketing and development for the Frito-Lay Company, an operating division of PepsiCo, Inc. that is engaged in the snack food industry, from 1999 to 2000; and vice president of corporate development at Pennzoil Quaker State Company, a manufacturer of automotive, commercial, industrial, and marine lubricants, from 1996 to 1999. Prior to 1996, she held various brand management positions with The Procter and Gamble Company, a global consumer products company.

Mr. Dunn joined the company in 1984 as assistant controller of inventory audit and control. He was named treasurer in 1990, was promoted to vice president in 1992 and added the title of controller in 1996. In 1999, he was elected senior vice president. Mr. Dunn was employed by Arthur Young & Co., an accounting firm and a predecessor of Ernst & Young LLP, from 1980 to 1984.

Mr. Jonas joined the company in 1998 as director of associate relations. He was promoted to assistant vice president of corporate human resources services in 1998 and was elected senior vice president in July 2004. Prior to joining the company, he was employed by Toys "R" Us, a worldwide retailer of toys, baby products, and children's apparel, from 1985 until 1998, including director of human resources for the Babies "R" Us division from 1996 to 1998.

Mr. Jones joined the company in 1999 as vice president, chief information officer, First North American National Bank. He was promoted to senior vice president, chief information officer in February 2004. Prior to joining the company, Mr. Jones was employed by Markel Corporation, an international property and casualty insurance holding company, for 10 years, most recently as president and chief operating officer of an operating subsidiary.

Mr. Mierenfeld joined the company in 1993 as vice president - distribution. He was elected senior vice president in 1999. He was named senior vice president - store development, procurement, distribution and service in 2003. Prior to joining the company, he was employed by The Gap, Inc., an international specialty retailer of clothing, accessories and personal care products, for 13 years in various human resources and distribution positions, including vice president of distribution. He was also employed by Sears, Roebuck and Co. for ten years in various management positions.

Mr. Moore joined the company in 1990 as a regional manager for the roadshop division. He was named a regional vice president in 1995; director of corporate operations in 1997; assistant vice president - general manager, builder appliance sales division in 1998; assistant vice president - senior national buyer in 1999; assistant vice president - divisional merchandising manager - imaging in 2000; assistant vice president - director of merchandising operations in 2002; Western Division president and senior vice president in 2003. In September 2004, Mr. Moore was named senior vice president, merchandising and in March 2005 he was named chief merchandising officer. Before joining the company, Mr. Moore was employed as a brand manager for AH Robins Company, Inc., a pharmaceuticals manufacturer, in its Dimetapp business from 1980 to 1985 and in various operational and marketing capacities for AMF Bowling, Inc., a global manufacturer and marketer of bowling products and operator of bowling centers, and Carnation Company.

Mr. Sieger joined the company in 2003 as vice president of warranty administration, with additional responsibility for the Service division including field and depot repair, installations, PC services and call centers. In March 2005, he was named senior vice president, general merchandise manager. Prior to joining the company, he spent 13 years at General Electric Company, a diversified technology, media and financial services company, working in roles in finance, marketing, e-commerce, sales and business development.

Mr. Speranza joined the company in April 2004 as senior vice president and chief marketing officer. Before joining the company, he was senior vice president - marketing and advertising, international at Toys "R" Us, Inc. from 1999 to 2003 and senior vice president – marketing and advertising at Toys "R" Us, Inc. from 1983 to 1999.

Mr. Wick joined the company in December 2004 as senior vice president, general merchandise manager for Audio and Video. Before joining the company, he served as executive vice president of Petters Group Worldwide, an independent operating company that specializes in brand marketing. Prior to joining Petters Group Worldwide in 2004, he was vice president of retail strategies at Best Buy. He joined Best Buy in 1996 and served as merchandising manager from 1996 to 2001 and as vice president of merchandise from 2001 to 2002. Before joining Best Buy, he worked for Fretter/Silo, formerly a large retailer of home entertainment products, consumer electronics and appliances, for ten years.

PART II

Item 5. Market for the Company's Common Equity, Related Shareholder Matters and Issuer Purchases of Equity Securities.

As of March 31, 2005, there were 6,612 shareholders of record of common stock. The common stock of Circuit City Stores, Inc. is traded on the New York Stock Exchange under the symbol CC.

	Market Price of Common Stock				Dividends	
	2005		2004			
Quarter	High	Low	High	Low	2005	2004
1st	$12.82	$10.18	$ 7.42	$3.91	$.0175	$.0175
2nd.	$14.30	$11.90	$10.44	$6.30	$.0175	$.0175
3rd	$17.87	$12.96	$13.21	$9.25	$.0175	$.0175
4th	$17.25	$13.40	$13.03	$8.69	$.0175	$.0175
Total					$.0700	$.0700

The following table provides information about common stock repurchases by or on behalf of the company during the quarter ended February 28, 2005:

(Amounts in millions except per share data)	Total Number of Shares Purchased	Average Price Paid per Share	Total Number of Shares Purchased as Part of Publicly Announced Program	Maximum Dollar Value of Shares that May Yet Be Purchased Under the Program*
December 1 – December 31, 2004	–	$ –	–	$105.6
January 1 – January 31, 2005	3.4	$13.86	3.4	$ 58.6
February 1 – February 28, 2005	0.2	$14.17	0.2	$ 55.8
Fiscal 2005 fourth quarter	3.6	$13.88	3.6	

**In January 2003, the company announced that the board of directors had authorized the repurchase of up to $200 million of common stock. In June 2004, the company announced a $200 million increase in its stock repurchase authorization, raising the repurchase capacity to $400 million. In March 2005, the company announced a $400 million increase in its stock repurchase authorization, raising the repurchase capacity to $800 million. There is no expiration date under the authorization. At March 31, 2005, $455.8 million remained available for share repurchases under the share repurchase authorization.*

If the remaining borrowing availability under the company's $500 million, four-year revolving credit facility falls below $100 million, cash dividends and stock repurchases are limited to an aggregate of $75 million in any fiscal year.

Item 6. Selected Financial Data.

	2005	2004	2003	2002	2001
CONSOLIDATED SUMMARY OF NET EARNINGS (LOSS) FROM CONTINUING OPERATIONS					
(Amounts in millions except per share data)					
Net sales and operating revenues	**$10,472**	$9,857	$ 10,055	$ 9,618	$10,445
Gross profit	**$ 2,569**	$2,284	$ 2,407	$ 2,383	$ 2,516
Earnings (loss) from continuing operations before income taxes	**$ 96**	$ (1)	$ (5)	$ 107	$ 137
Net earnings (loss) from continuing operations	**$ 60**	$ (1)	$ (5)	$ 68	$ 83
Net earnings (loss) per share from continuing operations:					
Basic	**$ 0.31**	$ —	$ (0.03)	$ 0.33	$ 0.41
Diluted	**$ 0.31**	$ —	$ (0.03)	$ 0.33	$ 0.41
CONSOLIDATED SUMMARY OF NET EARNINGS (LOSS) FROM CONTINUING OPERATIONS PERCENTAGES					
(% of sales except effective tax rate)					
Gross profit	**24.5**	23.2	23.9	24.8	24.1
Earnings (loss) from continuing operations before income taxes	**0.9**	—	(0.1)	1.1	1.3
Effective tax rate	**37.5**	36.5	3.3	36.7	38.9
Net earnings (loss) from continuing operations	**0.6**	—	(0.1)	0.7	0.8
CONSOLIDATED SUMMARY BALANCE SHEETS					
(Amounts in millions)					
Total current assets	**$ 2,686**	$2,919	$ 3,088	$ 3,653	$ 2,847
Property and equipment, net	**$ 739**	$ 677	$ 734	$ 819	$ 882
Long-term deferred income tax assets	**$ 74**	$ 88	$ 60	$ 26	$ 4
Other assets	**$ 44**	$ 46	$ 59	$ 175	$ 250
Goodwill and other intangible assets	**$ 247**	$ —	$ —	$ —	$ —
Total assets	**$ 3,789**	$3,731	$ 3,941	$ 4,672	$ 3,983
Total current liabilities	**$ 1,264**	$1,138	$ 1,229	$ 1,569	$ 1,228
Long-term debt, excluding current installments	**$ 12**	$ 23	$ 11	$ 14	$ 33
Other long-term liabilities	**$ 427**	$ 346	$ 327	$ 329	$ 348
Total liabilities	**$ 1,702**	$1,507	$ 1,567	$ 1,912	$ 1,610
Total stockholders' equity	**$ 2,087**	$2,224	$ 2,374	$ 2,761	$ 2,373
Total liabilities and stockholders' equity	**$ 3,789**	$3,731	$ 3,941	$ 4,672	$ 3,983
CONSOLIDATED SUMMARY OF CASH FLOWS FROM CONTINUING OPERATIONS					
(Amounts in millions)					
Depreciation and amortization	**$ 155**	$ 198	$ 160	$ 136	$ 128
Cash flow from operating activities of continuing operations	**$ 456**	$ (126)	$ (163)	$ 889	$ 88
Capital expenditures	**$ 269**	$ 176	$ 151	$ 173	$ 275
OTHER DATA					
Cash dividends per share paid	**$ 0.07**	$ 0.07	$ 0.07	$ 0.07	$ 0.07
Return on average stockholders' equity (%)*	**2.8**	—	(0.2)	2.6	3.7
Number of Associates of domestic segment	**42,425**	43,211	38,849	45,327	53,302
Number of Associates of international segment	**3,521**	—	—	—	—
Number of domestic segment retail stores	**617**	604	626	624	629
Number of international segment retail stores and dealer outlets	**966**	—	—	—	—

Results from continuing operations shown above exclude Digital Video Express, CarMax and the bankcard finance operation. All periods reflect the adoption of SFAS No. 123, as amended by SFAS No. 148. Consolidated results include results from InterTAN from the acquisition date, May 12, 2004. Results for fiscal 2005 include an after tax charge of $4.2 million for the cumulative impact of a revision to our lease accounting practices during the fourth quarter of fiscal 2005. Consolidated balance sheets reflect reclassifications as a result of revisions to our lease accounting practices. Consolidated results also reflect the reclassification of revenues, costs and expenses relating primarily to mobile audio installations for the domestic segment.

See consolidated financial statements and accompanying notes, included in Item 8, Financial Statement and Supplementary Data, of this Annual Report on Form 10-K.

*Calculated as earnings from continuing operations divided by average stockholders' equity.

Item 7. Management's Discussion and Analysis of Financial Condition and Results of Operations.

Management's Discussion and Analysis (MD&A) is designed to provide the reader of financial statements with a narrative discussion of our results of operations; financial position, liquidity and capital resources; critical accounting policies and significant estimates; and the impact of recently issued accounting standards. Our MD&A is presented in seven sections:

- Executive Summary
- Critical Accounting Policies
- Results of Operations
- Recent Accounting Pronouncements
- Financial Condition
- Fiscal 2006 Outlook
- Forward-Looking Statements

This discussion should be read in conjunction with the consolidated financial statements and accompanying notes included in this annual report. All per share amounts in this discussion are presented on a fully diluted basis.

Executive Summary

Fiscal 2005 Performance

We were pleased by the improvement in fiscal 2005 results compared with fiscal 2004.

- Net sales and operating revenues were $10.47 billion compared with $9.86 billion in the prior year, an increase of 6.2 percent. Comparable store sales grew 0.7 percent compared with a 1.2 percent decrease in fiscal 2004. The fiscal 2005 total sales increase reflects the inclusion of sales from the international segment, the net addition of 12 Superstores and the increase in comparable store sales.
- The gross profit margin increased by 136 basis points, from fiscal 2004, to 24.5 percent of sales. The inclusion of the international segment contributed 71 basis points to the improvement. In the domestic segment, an increase in extended warranty sales, which carry higher-than-average gross profit margins, and continued increases in the efficiency of our product service and distribution operations were partially offset by declines in merchandise margin, primarily due to high levels of promotional activities throughout much of the year.
- Selling, general and administrative expenses as a percent of sales were 23.5 percent in fiscal 2005, which was an increase of 36 basis points from the fiscal 2004 rate. The inclusion of the international segment increased the fiscal 2005 expense-to-sales ratio by 42 basis points. The expense ratio for the domestic segment declined slightly from the prior fiscal year as decreases in payroll, rent and occupancy, and remodel and relocation expenses were partially offset by increases in advertising and other expenses.
- Earnings before income taxes were 0.9 percent of sales in fiscal 2005 compared with 0 percent of sales in fiscal 2004. The inclusion of the international segment and improvements in the domestic gross profit margin primarily drove the increase.
- Earnings from continuing operations were $59.9 million, or 31 cents per share, compared with a net loss of $787,000, or 0 cents per share, in fiscal 2004. The improvement in net earnings from continuing operations in fiscal 2005 was driven by the inclusion of the international segment, increased domestic sales, improvements in domestic gross profit margin, and lower stock-based compensation expense, partially offset by higher selling, general and administrative expenses and reduced finance income.

Fiscal 2005 Significant Events

A number of our actions in fiscal 2005 demonstrated our continued commitment to maximizing shareholder value.

- *International expansion.* In May 2004, we completed our acquisition of InterTAN, Inc. for cash consideration of $259.3 million, which includes transaction costs and is net of cash acquired of $30.6 million. InterTAN is a leading consumer electronics retailer of both private-label and brand-name products with headquarters in Barrie, Ontario, Canada. In addition to giving us a greater product-sourcing capability and the ability to accelerate the offering of private-label merchandise to our customers, the acquisition of InterTAN gives us our first presence in the Canadian market.

- *Divestiture of private-label finance operation.* In May 2004, we completed the sale of our private-label finance operation, comprised of our private-label and co-branded Visa credit card programs, to Chase Card Services, formerly Bank One Corporation. Cash proceeds from the sale were $475.9 million.

  We entered into a Consumer Credit Card Program Agreement under which Chase Card Services is offering private-label and co-branded credit cards to new and existing customers. We are compensated under the program agreement primarily based on the number of new accounts opened less promotional financing costs that exceed a negotiated base amount. The earnings contribution from the Chase credit card program is included in net sales and operating revenues on the consolidated statement of operations.

- *Store revitalization.* The domestic segment opened 31 new stores, relocated 28 stores and fully remodeled one store. As of February 28, 2005, 189 stores, net of closings, or 31 percent of the store base, had been newly constructed, relocated or fully remodeled since the beginning of fiscal 2001. We also closed 19 Superstores, five regional offices and one distribution center in fiscal 2005, continuing our initiatives to improve our overall financial performance.

- *Share repurchase and dividends.* We repurchased 19.2 million shares of common stock for $259.8 million and paid $13.8 million in dividends during fiscal 2005.

- *Next-generation Web site launch.* In September 2004, we launched a next-generation Web site at www.circuitcity.com. The site, first launched in 1999, has been continuously upgraded over the years, but the re-launch represents circuitcity.com's first complete makeover. The new site features improved navigation; pioneering express pickup of merchandise in all of our stores; and, most importantly, award-winning customer service. We remain pleased with the strong growth in this profitable business.

- *Rejection of acquisition proposal.* During the year, Highfields Capital Management LP indicated interest in acquiring all of Circuit City's outstanding shares at a price of $17.00 in cash per share. The board of directors, after careful and thorough evaluation, unanimously determined that further exploring the transaction proposed by Highfields or other sale alternatives would not be in the best interests of our shareholders, and that we can best maximize shareholder value by continuing to aggressively implement the strategic, operational and financial initiatives currently under way and contemplated for the future.

Critical Accounting Policies

Our consolidated financial statements have been prepared in accordance with U.S. generally accepted accounting principles. Preparation of financial statements requires us to make estimates and assumptions affecting the reported amounts of assets, liabilities, revenues and expenses and the disclosures of contingent assets and liabilities. We use our historical experience and other relevant factors when developing our estimates and assumptions. We continually evaluate these estimates and assumptions. Note 2, Summary of Significant Accounting Policies, of the Notes to Consolidated Financial Statements, included in Item 8, Financial Statements and Supplementary Data, of this Annual Report on Form 10-K includes a discussion of our significant accounting policies. The following accounting policies are those we consider critical to an understanding of the consolidated financial statements because their application places the most significant demands on our judgment. Our financial results might have been different if other assumptions had been used or other conditions had prevailed.

Accounting for Cash Consideration Received from Vendors

We receive cash consideration from vendors through a variety of programs and arrangements, including cooperative advertising and vendor allowances. Given the promotional nature of our business, these vendor allowances are generally intended to offset our costs of promoting, advertising and selling the vendors' products in our stores. Inherent in the accounting for cash consideration received from vendors are significant management judgments and estimates, including the percentage of vendor allowances to be amortized to cost of sales, buying and warehousing and the percentage of vendor allowances that relate to inventory still on hand. We review these judgments and estimates on a monthly basis and make adjustments as appropriate.

We recognize the majority of vendor allowances as a reduction to cost of sales, buying and warehousing. Cash consideration received as part of cooperative advertising programs that represents a reimbursement of specific, incremental, identifiable direct costs incurred by us to advertise the vendors' products is reported as a reduction of advertising expense in the period in which the advertising occurs.

Calculation of the Liability for Lease Termination Costs

When leased properties are no longer used for operating purposes, we recognize a liability for remaining costs related to the properties, reduced by any contractual or estimated sublease income. Inherent in the calculation of accrued lease termination costs are significant management judgments and estimates, including estimates of future sublease revenues, vacancy periods, tenant improvement allowances, broker fees, taxes, insurance and maintenance costs, and the credit-adjusted risk-free interest rate used to discount the expected net cash payments. We review these judgments and estimates on a quarterly basis, and accrued lease termination costs is adjusted as appropriate. Fluctuations in the economy and in marketplace demand for commercial properties can result in material changes in the liability for lease termination costs.

Goodwill and Other Identified Intangible Assets

We evaluate goodwill for impairment on an annual basis, or more frequently if an event or circumstance indicates that the asset may be impaired. Goodwill, other intangible assets, and tangible assets and liabilities are divided among reporting units. The fair value of the reporting units is compared to the carrying value to determine if there is an indication that potential impairment may exist.

The performance of the goodwill impairment test is subject to significant judgment in determining the fair value of reporting units, the estimation of future cash flows, the estimation of discount rates, and other assumptions. Changes in these estimates and assumptions could have a significant impact on the fair value and/or goodwill impairment of each reporting unit.

Accounting for Stock-Based Compensation Expense

We account for stock-based compensation using a fair value-based method. The Black-Scholes option valuation model is used to determine the fair value of stock options at the date of grant and we recognize expense over the period in which the options vest. This valuation model was developed for use in estimating the fair value of traded options that do not have vesting restrictions and are fully transferable. Option valuation models require us to make highly subjective assumptions, including the expected future volatility of the stock price, expected dividend yield, risk-free interest rate and expected life of the option. Because the stock options granted have characteristics that are significantly different from those of traded options, and because changes in the subjective assumptions can materially affect the fair value estimate, the existing option valuation models, including the Black-Scholes model, do not necessarily provide a reliable single measure of the fair value of our employee stock options.

We have issued performance-based shares, which are considered restricted stock awards. The vesting of these shares is based upon the company achieving operating profit margin targets for fiscal 2006. Stock-based compensation expense related to the performance-based shares should be recognized based on the likelihood of management achieving the operating profit margin targets. The determination of our ability to achieve these targets requires management's judgment. During the fourth quarter of fiscal 2005, we determined that it is unlikely the performance targets related to the performance-based shares will be met. Accordingly, we reversed the compensation expense recorded to date.

Accounting for Pension Plans

Net pension expense recognized in our consolidated financial statements for our defined benefit pension plan and unfunded non-qualified benefit restoration plan is determined on an actuarial basis. The effects of both the performance of pension plan assets and changes in pension liability discount rates on the computation of net pension expense are amortized over future periods.

A significant element in determining the net pension expense is the expected return on plan assets. To develop the expected long-term rate of return assumption on our pension plan assets, we use historical long-term return experience, the expected investment mix of the plan's assets and estimates of future long-term investment returns. The rate of return assumption is reviewed annually and adjusted as appropriate. For fiscal 2005 and fiscal 2004, our expected rate of return on plan assets was 8.25 percent. Net pension expense for our pension plans was $19.8 million in fiscal 2005, $18.4 million in fiscal 2004 and $15.7 million in fiscal 2003. These expenses are included in selling, general and administrative expenses on the consolidated statements of operations.

At the end of each fiscal year, we determine the weighted average discount rate used to calculate the present value of plan liabilities. The discount rate is an estimate of the interest rate at which the pension liabilities could be effectively settled at the end of the year. When estimating the discount rate, we look to rates of return on high-quality, fixed-income investments that receive one of the two highest ratings given by a recognized rating agency. The weighted average discount rate was 5.75 percent at February 28, 2005, and 6.00 percent at February 29, 2004. The decline in our weighted average discount rate was due to the decline in market interest rates.

The rate of increase in compensation levels is another assumption used for determining net pension expense. We determine this rate based upon annual reviews of plan participants' historical levels of salary increases and expectations regarding potential future salary increases.

In October 2004, the board of directors approved an amendment to freeze both the pension and benefit restoration plans, effective February 28, 2005. As a result of the pension plan freeze, all eligible employees retain any benefits accumulated to the effective date, but are no longer eligible to increase their benefit. Eligible employees will continue to earn vesting credit toward the pension plan's vesting requirements. Employees who would be eligible to retire under both plans' early or normal retirement provisions on or before February 28, 2008, are considered grandfathered employees and are not subject to the plan changes. The impact of the plan changes is a curtailment charge of $1.1 million in the fiscal year ended February 28, 2005.

Income Taxes

Many deductions for tax return purposes are taken when the expenses are actually paid, rather than when the expenses are recorded for book purposes. We accrue for the tax benefit expected to be received in future years if, in our judgment, it is more likely than not that we will receive such benefits. The amount and timing of certain current deductions require interpretation of tax laws. We estimate and accrue income tax contingencies for differences in interpretation that may exist with tax authorities. We also periodically evaluate income tax contingency accruals and the likelihood the benefits of a deferred tax asset will be realized. We must consider a variety of factors, including the nature and amount of the tax income and expense items, the current tax statutes, the current status of audits performed by tax authorities and the projected future earnings.

Results of Operations

Lease Accounting Revision, Reclassifications and Change in Calculation of Comparable Store Sales

During the fourth quarter of fiscal 2005, we revised our accounting practices associated with leases, primarily related to landlord reimbursements for construction by us on leased property. To the extent that landlord reimbursements exceed structural costs of a new store, the excess of funding over cost is classified as a long-term liability. Shortfalls in funding result in capital expenditures for structural costs in excess of reimbursements from the landlord and the excess is classified as a long-term asset, unless the shortfall is substantial. In cases of substantial under-funding, the reimbursement is not used to offset capital expenditures; instead the entire amount is classified as a long-term liability.

Results for fiscal 2005 include an after tax charge of $4.2 million for the cumulative impact of a revision to our lease accounting practices. This adjustment does not impact historical or future net cash flows or the timing of any payments under the related leases. The accounting revision also affected the historical balance sheets. For 2005, the impact to property and equipment was an increase of $113.0 million, the impact to other assets was an increase of $15.1 million, the impact to deferred income taxes was an increase of $2.4 million, the impact to accrued straight-line rent and deferred rent expense was an increase of $134.6 million and the impact to retained earnings was a decrease of $4.2 million. For 2004, the impact to property and equipment was an increase of $91.2 million, the impact to other assets was an increase of $17.1 million and the impact to accrued straight-line rent and deferred rent expense was an increase of $108.3 million.

During the fourth quarter of fiscal 2005, we reclassified revenues, costs and expenses relating primarily to mobile audio installations for the domestic segment. These items, which were previously presented on a net basis as an offset to selling, general and administrative expenses, are now presented on a gross basis. The impact on the consolidated statement of operations for fiscal 2004 is an increase to revenues of $111.6 million, or 1 percent, offset by increases to cost of sales of $54.9 million, or 1 percent, and selling, general and administrative expenses of $56.7 million, or 3 percent. The impact on the consolidated statement of operations for fiscal 2003 is an increase to revenues of $101.3 million, or 1 percent, offset by increases to cost of sales of $44.8 million, or 1 percent, and selling, general and administrative expenses of $56.5 million, or 2 percent.

During the fourth quarter of fiscal 2005, we updated our calculation of comparable store sales to more accurately reflect business trends, including the growing importance of service-related revenues. We expanded the revenues included in comparable store sales to include extended warranties, installations and other non-merchandise revenues. Previously, revenues included in the comparable store sales calculation were limited to merchandise sales. Comparable store sales results have been presented to reflect the new calculation methodology.

Summary of Segment Performance

Where relevant, we have included separate discussions of our domestic and international segments. Our domestic segment is primarily engaged in the business of selling brand-name consumer electronics, personal computers, entertainment software and services in our Superstores and mall-based stores in the United States and via the Web at www.circuitcity.com. Our international segment is primarily engaged in the business of selling private-label and brand-name consumer electronics products in Canada and principally includes the operations of InterTAN, Inc., which we acquired in May 2004. Consolidated results include results from InterTAN from the acquisition date. Prior to the second quarter of fiscal 2005, we had a third reportable segment, our finance operation. The table below provides a summary of performance by segment.

SEGMENT PERFORMANCE SUMMARY

(Amounts in millions)	Domestic	International	Finance	Consolidated
	Year Ended February 28, 2005			
Net sales and operating revenues	$10,017.5	$454.9	$ –	$10,472.4
Gross profit	$ 2,386.2	$182.6	$ –	$ 2,568.7
Finance income	$ –	$ –	$5.6	$ 5.6
Selling, general and administrative expenses	$ 2,308.4	$148.6	$ –	$ 2,457.0
Earnings from continuing operations before income taxes	$ 57.8	$ 32.4	$5.6	$ 95.8

In fiscal 2004 and fiscal 2003 we had two reportable segments: our domestic retail operation and our finance operation. Finance income is presented as a separate line on the consolidated statements of operations, therefore no segment performance table is presented for these years.

Net Sales and Operating Revenues

Consolidated

For the fiscal year ended February 28, 2005, our total sales increased 6.2 percent to $10.47 billion, and comparable store sales increased 0.7 percent. In fiscal 2004, total sales decreased 2.0 percent to $9.86 billion from $10.05 billion in fiscal 2003, and comparable store sales decreased 1.2 percent.

PERCENT SALES CHANGE FROM PRIOR YEAR

Fiscal	Total	Comparable
2005	6.2%	0.7%
2004	(2.0)%	(1.2)%
2003	4.5%	0.9%

A store's sales are included in comparable store sales after the store has been open for a full 12 months. In addition, comparable store sales include all Web-originated sales and sales from relocated stores. Sales from closed stores are included in comparable store sales until the month in which the stores are closed. Comparable store sales for fiscal 2005 and total sales for fiscal 2004 and 2003 reflect domestic sales only.

The fiscal 2005 total sales increase reflects sales from the international segment, the addition of 31 Superstores and the increase in comparable store sales, partially offset by the closure of 19 Superstores in late fiscal 2004. In 2005 we believe we benefited from improved in-store execution in our domestic stores through most of the year, resulting in improvements in average ticket and extended warranty penetration rates for key merchandise classes. In February 2005, we closed 19 underperforming Superstores, which had sales of $170.5 million in fiscal 2005.

The fiscal 2004 total sales decrease reflects the decline in comparable store merchandise sales partly offset by the addition of eight Superstores. We believe our store-level execution, which was not consistent with our expectations, negatively impacted sales. This weak execution was reflected in an overall reduction in customer satisfaction levels. Higher-than-normal turnover in store-level management also contributed to the reduction in satisfaction levels. In February 2004, we closed 19 underperforming Superstores that had fiscal 2004 revenues of $149.9 million. We also closed one Superstore in advance of the planned opening of a replacement Superstore early in fiscal 2005.

Domestic Segment

The domestic segment's fiscal 2005 net sales and operating revenues were $10.02 billion, an increase of 1.6 percent over fiscal 2004 sales of $9.86 billion. Comparable store sales increased 0.7 percent. The sales increase reflects the addition of 31 Superstores and the comparable store sales gain, partially offset by the closure of 19 Superstores in late fiscal 2004.

PERCENT OF DOMESTIC MERCHANDISE SALES BY CATEGORY

	Years Ended February 28 or 29		
	2005	2004	2003
Video	42%	41%	40%
Information technology	31	32	32
Audio	14	13	15
Entertainment	13	14	13
Total	100%	100%	100%

For fiscal 2005, we generated strong comparable store sales growth in product categories with new technologies or improved functionality for the consumer: flat panel displays, including plasma and LCD technologies; large projection televisions; portable digital audio and accessories; digital camera and accessories; and digital satellite radio. Web-originated sales grew strongly throughout 2005. We experienced sales declines in mature product areas such as tube televisions, DVD players, home audio and telecommunications as well as a decline in sales of games products due to hardware inventory shortages.

In fiscal 2005 we experienced significant declines in revenues from two categories that experienced business model changes: wireless communications products and services and digital satellite services. The business model change for wireless communications reflects our strategic decision to add a Verizon store-within-a-store to more than 570 of our Superstores during the third quarter. Under the new business model, Verizon sells the products from its store-within-a-store and incurs the costs of labor, in-store signage and inventory. We receive and record revenues for each new handset activation within our store. The shift of product sales to Verizon negatively impacted our comparable store sales. We expect the added value of products and services to our customers will help drive additional traffic to our stores and contribute to stronger profitability in this business than could be achieved if we continued to operate it ourselves. The business model change for digital satellite services reflects a reduction in hardware subsidies paid to us by the service provider, resulting in lower revenues, and a reduction in hardware costs.

For fiscal 2004, we generated strong comparable store sales growth in digital imaging products and accessories; LCD and plasma display devices; digital televisions, including slim-line technologies; notebook computers; and the traffic-driving movies and music software categories. Web-originated sales also grew strongly throughout fiscal 2004.

Extended Warranty Revenues. The percent of total domestic sales attributable to sales of extended warranties was 3.8 percent in fiscal 2005, 3.3 percent in fiscal 2004 and 3.6 percent in fiscal 2003.

The domestic segment sells extended warranty programs on behalf of unrelated third parties who are the primary obligors. Extended warranty sales carry higher-than-average gross profit margins.

The increase in extended warranty sales as a percentage of total sales in fiscal 2005 compared with fiscal 2004 reflects improved in-store execution resulting from increased attention and training. This improvement offset the effects of declining average retail prices and rapid technological developments, both of which encourage consumers to replace products rather than purchase warranties that would cover future repairs. We continue to focus on our performance in this area, but as we approach historical levels, we expect that any increase in the percentage of total sales will be less than that achieved in fiscal 2005.

The decline in extended warranty sales as a percentage of total sales from fiscal 2003 to fiscal 2004 primarily reflects the declines in average retails and rapid technological developments and weak in-store execution, resulting, we believe, from a substantial increase in part-time sales Associates prior to our peak selling season.

Net Credit Revenues. In May 2004, we sold our private-label finance operation to Chase Card Services, formerly Bank One. We entered into an arrangement under which Chase offers private-label and co-branded credit cards to both new and existing customers. Revenues from new account activations are offset by the cost associated with promotional financing over a predetermined base. The earnings contribution from the program is included in net sales and operating revenues on the consolidated statement of operations. Net credit revenues for fiscal 2005 were $7.8 million.

From inception of the program in May 2004 through the end of the fiscal year, both the number of new account activations and the cost associated with promotional financing under the program exceeded our expectations. In the third quarter, we made a decision to offer financing promotions that were competitive in the marketplace, both in number of offers and durations of offers, which contributed to the higher-than-expected costs. As a result of the deviation from our original plan, pretax earnings generated were less than the $30 million that we had expected to generate annually when we entered into the sale arrangement.

DOMESTIC STORE MIX

	Retail Units at Year-end		
Fiscal	2005	2004	2003
Superstores	612	599	611
Mall-based stores	5	5	15
Total domestic segment stores	617	604	626

DOMESTIC SUPERSTORE SQUARE FOOTAGE SUMMARY

Fiscal	Selling Sq. Ft.	Total Sq. Ft.	Sales per Total Sq. Ft.
2005	12,953,259	20,922,618	$479
2004	12,063,551	20,133,411	$490
2003	12,003,045	20,271,427	$496

International Segment

The international segment net sales and operating revenues were $454.9 million in fiscal 2005. In addition to the 966 retail stores and dealer outlets, the international segment conducts business through 64 wholesale relationships.

INTERNATIONAL STORE MIX

	February 28, 2005
RadioShack stores	521
Dealer outlets	331
Rogers Plus stores	88
Battery Plus stores	26
Total international segment stores	966

Gross Profit Margin

Consolidated

The gross profit margin was 24.5 percent in fiscal 2005, 23.2 percent in fiscal 2004, and 23.9 percent in fiscal 2003. The higher gross profit margin in fiscal 2005 primarily reflects the inclusion of the international segment, increased extended warranty sales and increased efficiency in our product service and distribution operations, partially offset by declines in merchandise margin due to high levels of promotional activities throughout much of the year. The inclusion of the international segment contributed 71 basis points to the improvement.

The lower gross profit margin in fiscal 2004, compared with fiscal 2003, primarily reflects reductions in extended warranty sales during the first nine months and, in the fourth quarter, heavy promotions, particularly in December, on desktop personal computers; aggressive industry pricing on big-screen and advanced televisions; and some shifts in the merchandise mix to lower margin products. Reduced service and distribution costs partly offset these factors.

Domestic Segment

The domestic segment's gross profit margin increased 65 basis points in fiscal 2005 from fiscal 2004. The change in the domestic gross profit margin reflects an increase in extended warranty sales and increased efficiency in our product service and distribution operations, partially offset by declines in merchandise margin due to high levels of promotional activities throughout much of the year.

Prior to fiscal 2005, we did not have an international segment. Please refer to the discussion of consolidated results for factors contributing to prior years' performance.

International Segment

The international segment's gross profit margin in fiscal 2005 was 40.1 percent of international sales.

Finance Income

Finance income was $5.6 million in fiscal 2005, compared with $32.7 million in fiscal 2004 and $27.3 million in fiscal 2003. Finance income for fiscal 2005 includes a portion of the loss on the sale of the private-label finance operation to Chase Card Services and the income generated by the private-label finance operation from the beginning of the fiscal year through the sale date. The fiscal 2004 increase in finance income from fiscal 2003 resulted from the introduction of the co-branded feature to the private-label card, which allowed cardholders to make additional purchases outside of Circuit City. This feature led to increased purchase activity, little of which carried promotional interest rates. It also resulted in interchange income and cash advance fees, neither of which was earned before the co-branded feature was introduced.

Prior to November 2003, both our bankcard finance operation and our private-label finance operation were conducted through our wholly owned subsidiary, First North American National Bank, which was a limited-purpose credit card bank, and through consolidated special purpose subsidiaries and off-balance-sheet qualifying special purpose entities. As part of a focus on strengthening the financial performance of our core business, we sold our bankcard finance operation to FleetBoston Financial in November 2003 and sold our private-label finance operation to Chase Card Services in May 2004.

Results from the bankcard finance operation are presented as results from discontinued operations on the consolidated financial statements; therefore, its results are not included in the "Components of Finance Income" table. See "Net Earnings (Loss) from Discontinued Operations."

Coincident with the sale of the private-label operation to Chase, we entered into an ongoing arrangement with Chase under which they offer private-label and co-branded credit cards to both new and existing customers. Results from that arrangement are included in net sales and operating revenues on the consolidated statement of operations.

COMPONENTS OF FINANCE INCOME

(Amounts in millions)	2005	2004	2003
	Years Ended February 28 or 29		
Securitization income	$ 28.1	$120.9	$107.3
Less: Payroll and fringe benefit expenses	7.6	29.5	30.8
Other direct expenses	14.9	58.7	49.2
Finance income	$ 5.6	$ 32.7	$ 27.3

Securitization income primarily is comprised of the gain on the sale of the credit card receivables, income from the retained interests in the securitized receivables and income related to servicing the securitized receivables, as well as the impact of increases or decreases in the fair value of the retained interests.

Selling, General and Administrative Expenses

Consolidated

SELLING, GENERAL AND ADMINISTRATIVE EXPENSES

	Years Ended February 28 or 29					
	2005		2004		2003	
(Dollar amounts in millions)	$[(a)]	% of Sales	$	% of Sales	$	% of Sales
Store expenses	$2,188.9	20.9%	$2,018.8	20.5%	$2,111.7	21.0%
General and administrative expenses	225.6	2.2	202.3	2.1	226.4	2.2
Remodel expenses	0.3	-	23.9	0.2	28.8	0.3
Relocation expenses	40.8	0.4	30.5	0.3	19.1	0.2
Pre-opening expenses	15.8	0.1	8.6	0.1	7.2	0.1
Interest income	(14.4)	(0.1)	(6.6)	(0.1)	(7.9)	(0.1)
Total	$2,457.0	23.5%	$2,277.5	23.1%	$2,385.3	23.7%

(a) Includes international segment store expenses of $121.0 million and general and administrative expenses of $28.0 million.

Selling, general and administrative expenses were 23.5 percent of sales in fiscal 2005, 23.1 percent of sales in fiscal 2004, and 23.7 percent of sales in fiscal 2003.

The increase in the selling, general and administrative expense ratio from fiscal 2004 to fiscal 2005 reflects the inclusion of the international segment, which increased the fiscal 2005 expense-to-sales ratio by 42 basis points. Domestic selling, general and administrative expenses were approximately flat to the prior year as a percent of sales as lower payroll and rent and occupancy expenses were offset by various increased costs. The fiscal 2005 expenses include costs of $47.4 million related to the closing of 19 Superstores and five regional offices during the year, an expense of $6.5 million for the cumulative impact of a multi-year lease accounting revision and a gain of $2.8 million related to the sale of one of our corporate office buildings. The fiscal 2005 expenses include costs associated with 28 relocations, as well as accelerated depreciation of assets related to planned future relocations, and costs associated with fully remodeling one Superstore.

The reduction in the selling, general and administrative expense ratio from fiscal 2003 to fiscal 2004 largely reflects lower store operating costs, resulting primarily from reductions in comparable store payroll, and a reduction in advertising expenses. Store-related payroll savings of approximately $130 million from comparable stores were driven primarily by the change, initiated in February 2003, in the store compensation structure. The fiscal 2004 expenses include costs of $38.4 million related to the closing of 19 Superstores during the year and a $5.9 million benefit resulting from a reduction in liabilities associated with our gift card program. The fiscal 2003 expenses included $10.0 million related to the change in our store compensation structure in February of that year. The fiscal 2004 expenses include costs associated with 18 relocations, as well as accelerated depreciation of assets related to planned future relocations, and costs associated with fully remodeling four Superstores and refixturing 222 Superstores. Remodel expenses incurred in fiscal 2004 include $21.7 million for refixturing.

Domestic Segment

The domestic segment's expense-to-sales ratio decreased six basis points in fiscal 2005 from fiscal 2004. The slight decrease resulted from lower payroll and rent and occupancy expenses offset by increases in advertising and other costs. Relocation and remodel expenses totaled $41.1 million in fiscal 2005 compared with $54.4 million in fiscal 2004 and $47.9 million in fiscal 2003.

Prior to fiscal 2005, we did not have an international segment. Please refer to the discussion of consolidated results for factors contributing to prior years' performance.

International Segment

The international segment's selling, general and administrative expenses for fiscal 2005 were 32.7 percent of international segment sales.

Stock-based Compensation Expense

Stock-based compensation expense was $19.4 million in fiscal 2005, compared with $38.7 million in fiscal 2004 and $53.3 million in fiscal 2003.

The decrease in stock-based compensation expense from fiscal 2004 to fiscal 2005 reflects lower weighted-average fair values of recent grants and the full vesting of grants during the year. The decrease also reflects a reversal of previously recognized compensation costs related to performance-based restricted stock grants. Under the terms of the restricted stock grant, vesting is contingent upon our achieving a targeted operating profit margin for fiscal 2006. During the fourth quarter, management determined that it is unlikely that the target will be met and, as a result, reversed the expense recorded to date.

The decrease in stock-based compensation expense from fiscal 2003 to fiscal 2004 reflects lower weighted-average fair values of recent grants and the full vesting of grants during the year.

Income Tax Provision

The consolidated effective income tax rate applicable to results from continuing operations in fiscal 2005 was 37.5 percent compared with 36.5 percent in fiscal 2004. The increase in the rate in fiscal 2005 reflects the inclusion of the international segment. In fiscal 2005, the effective income tax rate applicable to results from continuing operations for our domestic segment was 36.6 percent and 39.2 percent for our international segment.

The consolidated effective income tax rate applicable to results from continuing operations was 3.3 percent in fiscal 2003 compared with 36.5 percent in fiscal 2004. The low rate in fiscal 2003 is the result of state income taxes and nondeductible items

Net Earnings (Loss) from Continuing Operations

Net earnings from continuing operations were $59.9 million, or 31 cents per share, for the fiscal year ended February 28, 2005. The net loss from continuing operations was $787,000, or 0 cents per share, for the fiscal year ended February 29, 2004, compared with $5.3 million, or 3 cents per share, for the fiscal year ended February, 28, 2003.

The improvement in net earnings from continuing operations in fiscal 2005 was driven by the inclusion of the international segment, increased domestic sales, improvements in domestic gross profit margin, and lower stock-based compensation expenses, partially offset by higher selling, general and administrative expenses and reduced finance income. The international segment's results increased net earnings from continuing operations for fiscal year 2005 by $19.7 million, or 10 cents per share.

In fiscal 2004, the improvement in finance income and the reduction in selling, general and administrative expenses drove the slight improvement in performance from fiscal 2003.

Net Earnings (Loss) from Discontinued Operations

NET EARNINGS (LOSS) FROM DISCONTINUED OPERATIONS

	Years Ended February 28 or 29		
(Amounts in millions)	2005	2004	2003
Bankcard business	$(1.2)	$(90.0)	$25.6
CarMax	–	–	62.0
Divx	3.0	1.5	–
Net earnings (loss) from discontinued operations	$ 1.7	(88.5)	$87.6

On November 18, 2003, we completed the sale of our bankcard operation to FleetBoston Financial. Results from the bankcard operation are presented as results from discontinued operations.

On October 1, 2002, we completed the separation of the CarMax auto superstore business from our consumer electronics business. CarMax results are presented as results from discontinued operations.

In fiscal 2000, we ceased marketing the Divx home video system and discontinued that business. Operating results of Divx and the loss on the disposal of the business have been presented as results from discontinued operations. In the fourth quarter of fiscal 2005, we reduced the provision for commitments under Divx license agreements, resulting in a $3.0 million after-tax gain. We have no further commitments related to the Divx operation. In fiscal 2004, we reduced the provision for commitments under licensing agreements, resulting in a $1.5 million after-tax benefit to the net loss from discontinued operations.

Recent Accounting Pronouncements

In December 2004, the Financial Accounting Standards Board issued Statement of Financial Accounting Standards No. 123 (revised 2004), "Share-Based Payment." SFAS No. 123(R) requires companies to record compensation expense based on the fair value of employee stock-based compensation awards. The statement also requires that the compensation expense be recognized over the period during which the employee is required to provide service in exchange for the award. SFAS No. 123(R) will be effective for our first quarter of fiscal 2007. We have not yet determined the impact of adopting this standard. See Note 15(A), Stock-Based Incentive Plans, of the Notes to Consolidated Financial Statements, included in Item 8, Financial Statements and Supplementary Data, of this Annual Report on Form 10-K for information regarding our adoption of SFAS No. 123.

Financial Condition

Liquidity and Capital Resources

Operating Activities

We generated net cash of $455.9 million from operating activities in fiscal 2005, compared with uses of net cash from operating activities of $125.5 million in fiscal 2004 and $163.1 million in fiscal 2003.

The generation of cash resulted from improved working capital management as domestic merchandise inventory levels were reduced from the prior year and accounts payable increased from the prior year. Accounts payable were 66 percent of merchandise inventories at February 28, 2005, up from 55 percent of inventories at February 29, 2004.

The largest use of cash in fiscal 2004 was a $186.5 million increase in retained interests in securitized private-label credit card receivables. This increase was driven by higher subordinated retained interests required for the private-label securitization transactions that were completed in early fiscal 2004. In fiscal 2005, we sold the private-label finance operation, eliminating the securitization program. In fiscal 2004, we also used cash to help fund a $107.5 million increase in merchandise inventory. Accounts payable declined $85.7 million, to 55 percent of inventory at February 29, 2004, as we slowed purchasing activity in the last two months of the fiscal year to correct our inventory levels following lower-than-anticipated December sales.

Investing Activities

In fiscal 2005, we sold our private-label finance operation. Cash proceeds from the sale were $475.9 million. In May 2004, we acquired the operations of InterTAN, Inc. for $259.3 million, net of acquired cash of $30.6 million. In fiscal 2005, we purchased investment securities of $125.3 million.

Gross capital expenditures were $269.2 million in fiscal 2005, $175.8 million in fiscal 2004 and $150.8 million in fiscal 2003. Capital expenditures have been funded primarily through available cash, landlord reimbursements and sale-leaseback transactions. Net of proceeds from the sales of property and equipment, which include landlord reimbursements qualifying as sale-leaseback transactions, capital expenditures were $162.8 million in fiscal 2005, $135.3 million in fiscal 2004 and $90.9 million in fiscal 2003.

Landlord reimbursements of $11.0 million in fiscal 2005, $6.2 million in fiscal 2004 and $1.0 million in fiscal 2003 are considered tenant improvement allowances and included in cash flows from operating activities on the consolidated statements of cash flows.

Capital expenditures, net of total landlord reimbursements, for fiscal 2005 totaled $164 million and included

- $56 million related to relocations and one full remodel,
- $42 million related to new store construction,
- $37 million related to information systems,
- $21 million related to store, distribution and other expenses and
- $8 million related to the international segment.

We expect that available cash, landlord reimbursements and sale-leaseback transactions will be sufficient to fund capital expenditures for the foreseeable future.

Financing Activities

In January 2003, the board of directors authorized the repurchase of up to $200 million of common stock. In June 2004, the board authorized a $200 million increase in the authorization, raising the total repurchase capacity to $400 million. In March 2005, the board of directors authorized a $400 million increase in our stock repurchase authorization, raising the total repurchase capacity to $800 million. The repurchases may be made from time to time in the open market, with the price to be paid and the timing of purchases at the discretion of management. During fiscal 2005, we repurchased 19.2 million shares at a cost of $259.8 million. During fiscal 2004, we repurchased 9.3 million shares at a cost of $84.4 million. We did not repurchase any common stock in fiscal 2003. Based on the market value of the common stock at March 31, 2005, the remaining $455.8 million authorized would allow for the repurchase of up to approximately 15 percent of the 188 million shares then outstanding.

At February 28, 2005, outstanding debt totaled $12.4 million, compared with $23.8 million at February 29, 2004, and $12.7 million at February 28, 2003. We leased a corporate office building under an operating lease arrangement with a variable interest entity. The adoption of FASB Interpretation No. 46 required us to report the building and related debt on the consolidated balance sheet, resulting in the year-over-year increase in long-term debt from fiscal 2003 to fiscal 2004. In fiscal 2005, we sold the corporate office building and the related debt was paid in full.

On June 27, 2003, we entered into a $500 million, four-year revolving credit facility secured by inventory and accounts receivable. This facility is used to support letters of credit and for short-term borrowing needs. Loans primarily bear interest at a spread over LIBOR or at prime. The facility is scheduled to mature in June 2007 and provides for a one-year extension. The maximum credit extensions, including loans and outstanding letters of credit, permitted under the credit facility on any date are determined by calculating a borrowing base that is a percentage of our eligible inventory and accounts receivable as of the date of the credit extension. If the borrowing availability under the facility falls below $100 million, cash dividends and stock repurchases are limited to an aggregate of $75 million in any fiscal year. If the borrowing availability under the facility falls below $50 million for five consecutive business days, all proceeds from the sale of inventory must be applied on a daily basis to payment of amounts owed under the facility. The facility has representations and warranties, covenants and events of default that are customary for this type of credit facility. On July 8, 2004, the credit agreement was amended to include InterTAN as a borrower. The amended credit agreement established a $400 million borrowing limit for the domestic segment and a $100 million borrowing limit for the international segment. At February 28, 2005, we had no short-term borrowings under the facility. At February 28, 2005, outstanding letters of credit related to this facility were $56.2 million, leaving $443.8 million available for borrowing. We were in compliance with all covenants at February 28, 2005.

In fiscal 2003, we used working capital to repay a $100 million outstanding term loan at its scheduled maturity date. At the payment date, $22.2 million of outstanding debt had been allocated to Circuit City and is included in payments on long-term debt on the consolidated statement of cash flows for the fiscal year ended February 28, 2003. The remaining balance had been allocated to CarMax and is included in cash used in discontinued operations on the consolidated statement of cash flows for the fiscal year ended February 28, 2003.

Cash, Cash Equivalents and Short-term Investments

At February 28, 2005, we had cash, cash equivalents and short-term investments of $1.00 billion, compared with cash and cash equivalents of $783.5 million at February 29, 2004, and $884.7 million at February 28, 2003. Cash generated by operating activities, the $475.9 million in cash proceeds received at the closing of the sales of the private-label finance operation and improvements in working capital management were partly offset by acquisition costs for InterTAN of $259.3 million, net of cash acquired, and stock repurchases of $259.8 million.

Our primary sources of liquidity include available cash, borrowing capacity under the credit facility, landlord reimbursements and sale-leaseback transactions.

Potential uses of cash during fiscal 2006 include

- capital expenditures, primarily for new and relocating stores and information technology systems;
- purchases of merchandise inventory;
- payment of dividends;
- expansion of our Web business;
- innovation initiatives;
- repurchases of common stock; and
- acquisitions that would support the initiatives in our core business.

Domestic Store Revitalization Program

From the beginning of fiscal 2001 through February 28, 2005, we built as new, relocated or fully remodeled 189 stores, net of closings, as part of an overall effort to bring a more contemporary shopping experience to our customers. In addition to new store designs, we have increased inventory levels on the sales floor in virtually all stores to help ensure that customers find complete consumer electronics solutions, including all the accessories they need.

During fiscal 2005, the domestic segment opened 59 Superstores and fully remodeled one Superstore. Twenty-eight of the opened stores were relocations and 31 were incremental stores. Expenses related to domestic store relocations and one remodel totaled $41.1 million in fiscal 2005.

Since the initiation of our store revitalization program at the beginning of fiscal 2001 through the end of fiscal 2005, the domestic segment has relocated 66 stores, of which 46 have been open for more than six months. In their first full six months following grand opening, these stores had

- an average sales change that was approximately 28 percentage points better than the sales pace of the remainder of the store base during the same time periods and
- an internal rate of return of approximately 15 percent.

The 31 relocated stores open more than 12 months produced the following results for their 12-month periods after grand opening:

- an average sales change that was approximately 25 percentage points better than the sales pace of the remainder of the store base during the same time periods;
- a return on invested capital, including lease termination and sublease costs on vacated stores, of approximately 7 percent; and
- a return on invested capital, excluding lease termination and sublease costs on vacated stores, of approximately 18 percent.

The reported return on invested capital performance for relocated stores open more than 12 months includes the impact of terminating the leases on, rather than subleasing, three of the four stores added to the calculation base in the fourth quarter of fiscal 2005. In most cases when terminating a lease, the aggregate payout to the landlord would be less than the aggregate payout to the landlord, net of sublease income, over the life of a sublease. Due to the timing of the payment, however, the return on invested capital in the measured period is lower under a lease termination, in which a one-time payment is made, than under a sublease, in which the payments are spread over the life of the lease.

Since initiation of the revitalization program in fiscal 2001, the domestic segment has opened 80 incremental stores. For the measured periods, incremental stores have produced the following results:

- a return on invested capital of approximately 13 percent measured at the end of the first twelve months after grand opening for the 48 stores that have been open for more than 12 months and
- a return on invested capital of approximately 22 percent measured at the end of the second twelve months after grand opening for the 41 stores that have been open for more than 24 months.

We anticipate that, as stores are added to the relocation base and incremental store base, the average results from relocated and incremental stores will vary.

We remain committed to our store revitalization strategy. As we build stores, we are committed to selecting superior real estate, and so, the mix of new versus relocated stores opened in any one year will depend upon the availability of sites that we expect would meet or exceed management's performance hurdles.

Contractual Obligations

CONTRACTUAL OBLIGATIONS AT FEBRUARY 28, 2005

(Amounts in millions)	Total	1 Year	2 to 3 Years	4 to 5 Years	After 5 Years
Contractual obligations:					
Capital leases	$ 12.4	$ 0.9	$ 2.2	$ 2.8	$ 6.5
Operating leases	5,077.6	406.6	802.6	771.7	3,096.7
Other contractual obligations [(a)]	183.2	53.7	49.6	41.1	38.7
Total	$5,273.2	$461.2	$854.4	$815.6	$3,141.9

(a) Other contractual obligations include commitments related to information technology programs, advertising and outsourcing.

CarMax currently operates 23 of its sales locations pursuant to leases under which we are the primary obligor. We rather than CarMax, entered into these leases so that CarMax could take advantage of the favorable economic terms available to us as a large retailer. We have assigned each of these leases to CarMax, but we remain contingently liable under the leases. In recognition of our ongoing contingent liability, CarMax paid a $28.4 million special dividend to us at the time of the separation in fiscal 2003. At February 28, 2005, the future minimum fixed lease obligations on these 23 leases totaled $422.9 million and are included in operating leases in the above table.

Off-Balance Sheet Arrangements

We do not have any off-balance sheet arrangements at February 28, 2005.

Fiscal 2006 Outlook

Despite the improvements in operating results that we generated in fiscal 2005, comparable store sales and customer traffic were volatile over the course of the year. We understand that we must drive initiatives to strengthen our core business as well as transform the business to foster new growth opportunities, and we are taking aggressive actions to achieve those goals.

We expect to generate the following results in fiscal 2006:

- total sales growth of 3 percent to 6 percent, including domestic comparable store sales growth in the low single-digit range
- operating margin, which is earnings from continuing operations before income taxes, of 1.3 percent to 2.3 percent

Revenue and gross profit margin

Important opportunities and initiatives for revenue growth and increased gross profit margin include:

International segment. We acquired InterTAN, Inc. in May 2004. Segment sales in the first quarter of fiscal 2006 will be incremental total sales growth. We also expect growth in the business in the other three quarters, which would be reflected in comparable store sales growth.

Domestic store revitalization. We expect to open 30 to 40 new Superstores, of which slightly less than half are expected to be relocations, with the openings weighted toward the second half of the year. New store openings contribute to total sales, and sales from relocated stores contribute to comparable store sales growth.

Promotional effectiveness. This year we will invest in systems that provide a more accurate measure of the effectiveness of our advertising and promotions. Using feedback to create more effective advertising should have the benefit of driving incremental traffic and sales, improving close rates and improving our brand image with consumers.

Customer experience. Our focus on an improved customer experience includes improving store displays and the store layout, better associate engagement with the customer and enhanced customer perceived in-stock levels. These changes should increase the close rate and sales.

Circuit City Direct. We expect continued sales growth from our Circuit City Direct business, which includes www.circuitcity.com. Growth in our direct channel business contributes to comparable store sales growth.

Gap management. Another area of focus this year will be on reducing the size of the performance gap between our best and poorest performing stores. Depending on the area of measurement and our level of success, improving the performance of the poorest stores will generate sales, profits and cash.

Best sourcing. Our goal is to find the lowest priced products with the highest quality for customers. Depending on the type of product, we may procure merchandise from a variety of sources and methods, including new and existing vendors, reverse auctions and direct relationships with manufacturers. We also will use our global sourcing capability gained through the acquisition of InterTAN. We believe better sourcing will lead to lower procurement costs and better merchandise selection, which should boost sales.

Services. We currently offer many services to our customers, including narrowband, broadband, wireless telephone, voice-over IP, digital video services, extended warranty programs, satellite radio, computer upgrades and repairs, car audio installation and in-home video installation. We will continue to explore opportunities in service offerings, which we would expect to increase sales with gross margins above our average.

Assortment optimization and transition management. Through assortment optimization, we will refine the product offerings on a market-by-market and store-by-store basis. Tailoring assortments should allow us to reduce inventory exposure at low risk of missed sales and provide an integrated multi-channel offering allowing us to sell from circuitcity.com's broad assortment in our stores. During fiscal 2006, we also expect to improve our sales forecasting accuracy with better training and improved systems, providing for smoother product transitions with less need to mark down obsolete product. We believe our efforts will result in fewer markdowns, which would lead to higher sales dollars, gross profit dollars and cash.

Innovation. Beyond initiatives to improve our existing business, we will expand our opportunities in order to generate long-term sales growth. Innovation teams will generate many ideas; then we will pursue, develop and test concepts aimed at the creation of value and the transformation of our business for the future. We will take calculated risks and make fact-based decisions, ultimately adopting winning ideas. Opportunities identified and captured by this innovation process should contribute to a sustainable long-term growth rate, and in return, generate shareholder value growth.

Selling, General and Administrative Expenses

We expect that the majority of the operating margin improvement will come from increases in gross profit margin rather than improvements in the selling, general and administrative expense-to-sales ratio as we expect to invest in key improvements to our business to help position ourselves for improved profitability and future growth.

Expenses related to domestic store relocations are expected to total approximately $17 million.

Tax Rate

We expect the estimated effective income tax rate applicable to results from continuing operations for our domestic segment for fiscal 2006 will be 37.0 percent. We expect the estimated effective income tax rate applicable to results from continuing operations from our international segment for fiscal 2006 will be 39.1 percent. The consolidated effective income tax rate applicable to results from continuing operations will be the weighted average of our segments' rates.

Working Capital

In fiscal 2006 we plan to further reduce our net owned inventory – our inventory position net of accounts payable. We have brought in senior management talent to spearhead this focus. Reductions in net owned inventory generate cash, and we expect to make progress in this area of focus.

Capital Expenditures

We anticipate that capital expenditures, net of landlord reimbursements and sale leasebacks, for our domestic and international segments combined will total approximately $205 million in fiscal 2006. Of the fiscal 2006 estimate,

- $108 million relates to information systems;
- $69 million relates to the opening of 30 to 40 new store locations, of which slightly less than half are expected to be relocations;
- $20 million relates to the international segment; and
- $8 million relates to store, distribution and other expenditures.

During fiscal 2006 and fiscal 2007, we expect to make significant investments both to improve the tools and processes that we will use to transform our business and to create new growth engines. We will invest in a number of standards-based systems to replace the proprietary systems that we currently use. We expect to complete the implementation of our new point of sale system by the end of the fiscal year. We also will improve our view of data through a company-wide data warehouse. Other areas of focus will be in supply chain and customer data, merchandising and marketing systems and standardization of our infrastructure to simplify support. Once completed, the transformation will give us next generation systems that we expect will

- dramatically improve our infrastructures and the flow of information,
- be easier and less costly to maintain and
- facilitate cross-functional communication.

Expected impact of international segment litigation

We are engaged in litigation with RadioShack Corporation regarding early termination of the licensing, merchandising and advertising agreements with RadioShack. Because of the ongoing legal conflict with RadioShack, we have taken steps to position our Canadian operations for continued success, regardless of the outcome of this litigation. We expect to discontinue the use of the RadioShack name in Canada by June 30, 2005, by re-branding to "THE SOURCE BY CIRCUIT CITY."

Potential negative impacts of this transition include:

- sales disruption from replacing old brand
- expenses for advertising new brand, and
- capital expenditures and expenses for new store signage

Potential positive impacts of this transition include:

- sales benefit from excitement generated by new brand and
- discontinuation of payments to RadioShack of royalty and other fees

We believe this litigation will not have a material adverse effect on our financial condition or results of operations.

Forward-Looking Statements

The provisions of the Private Securities Litigation Reform Act of 1995 provide companies with a "safe harbor" when making forward-looking statements. This "safe harbor" encourages companies to provide prospective information about their companies without fear of litigation. We wish to take advantage of the "safe harbor" provisions of the Act. Our statements that are not historical facts, including statements about management's expectations for fiscal 2006 and beyond, are forward-looking statements and involve various risks and uncertainties. In most cases, you can identify our forward-looking statements by words such as "expect," "believe," "should," "may," "plan," "will" or similar words.

Forward-looking statements are estimates and projections reflecting our judgment and involve a number of risks and uncertainties that could cause actual results to differ materially from those suggested by the forward-looking statements. Although we believe that the estimates and projections reflected in the forward-looking statements are reasonable, our expectations may prove to be incorrect. The retail industry, and the specialty retail industry in particular, are dynamic by nature and have undergone significant changes in recent years. Our ability to anticipate and successfully respond to the continuing challenges of our industry is key to achieving our expectations. Important factors that could cause actual results to differ materially from estimates or projections contained in our forward-looking statements include

- changes in the amount and degree of competition and promotional pressure exerted by current competitors and potential new competition from competitors using either similar or alternative methods or channels of distribution such as the Internet, telephone shopping services and mail order;
- changes in general economic conditions including, but not limited to, financial market performance, consumer credit availability, interest rates, inflation, personal discretionary spending levels, trends in consumer retail spending, both in general and in our product categories, unemployment and consumer sentiment about the economy in general;
- the presence or absence of, or consumer acceptance of, new products or product features in the merchandise categories we sell and changes in our merchandise sales mix;
- the impact of new products and product features on the demand for existing products and the pricing and profit margins associated with the products we sell;
- significant changes in retail prices for products we sell;
- changes in availability or cost of financing for working capital and capital expenditures, including financing to support development of our business;
- the lack of availability or access to sources of inventory or the loss or disruption in supply from one of our major suppliers;
- the impact of inventory and supply chain management initiatives on inventory levels and profitability;
- our inability to liquidate excess inventory should excess inventory develop;
- failure to successfully implement sales and profitability improvement programs for our Circuit City Superstores, including our store revitalization plan;
- our ability to continue to generate strong sales growth through our Web site;
- the availability of appropriate real estate locations for relocations and new stores;
- the cost and timeliness of new store openings and relocations;
- consumer reaction to new store locations and changes in our store design and merchandise;
- our ability and the ability of Chase Card Services to successfully integrate our retail business with the third party credit card program being offered by Chase Card Services;
- the extent to which customers respond to promotional financing offers and the types of promotional terms we offer;
- future levels of sales activity and the acceptance of the Chase Card Services third party credit program, including the related rewards component, by consumers on an ongoing basis;
- our ability to attract and retain an effective management team or changes in the costs or availability of a suitable work force to manage and support our service-driven operating strategies;
- changes in production or distribution costs or costs of materials for our advertising;
- effectiveness of our advertising and marketing programs for increasing consumer traffic and sales;

- the successful implementation of our customer service initiatives;
- the imposition of new restrictions or regulations regarding the sale of products and/or services we sell, changes in tax rules and regulations applicable to us or our competitors, the imposition of new environmental restrictions, regulations or laws or the discovery of environmental conditions at current or future locations, or any failure to comply with such laws or any adverse change in such laws;
- our ability to integrate and operate InterTAN successfully and to realize the anticipated benefits of the transaction, including successfully introducing InterTAN's products in our domestic Superstores and realizing inventory purchasing synergies;
- the timely production and delivery of private-label merchandise and level of consumer demand for those products;
- reduced investment returns in our pension plan;
- changes in our anticipated cash flow;
- whether, when and in what amounts share repurchases may be made under our stock buyback program;
- adverse results in significant litigation matters;
- the ultimate outcome of the litigation instituted by RadioShack Corporation to terminate InterTAN's right to use the RadioShack® name in Canada and related rights to purchase merchandise through RadioShack, any associated costs, any change in competitive conditions, or any business disruption resulting from the rebranding of InterTAN's RadioShack branded stores and dealer outlets in Canada;
- currency exchange rate fluctuations between Canadian and U.S. dollars and other currencies;
- the regulatory and trade environment in the U.S. and Canada;
- the disruption of global, national or regional transportation systems;
- the occurrence of severe weather events or natural disasters which could significantly damage or destroy stores or prohibit consumers from traveling to our retail locations, especially during the peak holiday shopping season; and
- the successful execution of the initiatives to achieve revenue growth and increase gross profit margin underlying our projected 2006 results as discussed under "Fiscal 2006 Outlook" in MD&A.

We believe our forward-looking statements are reasonable. However, undue reliance should not be placed on forward-looking statements, which are based on current expectations.

Item 7A. Quantitative and Qualitative Disclosures about Market Risk.

As a result of the acquisition of InterTAN, we are exposed to market risk from potential changes in the U.S./Canadian currency exchange rates as they relate to inventory purchases and the translation of InterTAN's financial results.

Inventory Purchases

A portion of InterTAN's purchases are from vendors requiring payment in U.S. dollars. Accordingly, there is risk that the value of the Canadian dollar could fluctuate relative to the U.S. dollar from the time the goods are ordered until payment is made. InterTAN's management monitors the foreign exchange risk associated with its U.S. dollar open orders on a regular basis by reviewing the amount of such open orders, exchange rates, including forecasts from major financial institutions, local news and other economic factors. At February 28, 2005, U.S. dollar open purchase orders totaled approximately $22.6 million. A 10 percent decline in the value of the Canadian dollar would result in an increase in product cost of approximately $2.3 million for those orders. The incremental cost of such a decline in currency values, if incurred, would be reflected in higher cost of sales in future periods. In these circumstances, management would take product pricing action, to the degree commercially feasible.

Translation of Financial Results

Fluctuations in the value of the Canadian dollar have a direct effect on reported consolidated results due to the acquisition of InterTAN. We do not hedge against the possible impact of this risk. A 10 percent adverse change in the foreign currency exchange rate would not have a significant impact on our results of operations or financial position.

Item 8. Financial Statements and Supplementary Data.

CONSOLIDATED STATEMENTS OF OPERATIONS

(Amounts in thousands except per share data)	Years Ended February 28 or 29 2005	%	2004	%	2003	%
NET SALES AND OPERATING REVENUES	**$10,472,364**	**100.0**	$9,857,057	100.0	$10,054,864	100.0
Cost of sales, buying and warehousing	**7,903,641**	**75.5**	7,573,049	76.8	7,647,992	76.1
GROSS PROFIT	**2,568,723**	**24.5**	2,284,008	23.2	2,406,872	23.9
Finance income	**5,564**	**0.1**	32,693	0.3	27,292	0.3
Selling, general and administrative expenses	**2,457,032**	**23.5**	2,277,479	23.1	2,385,310	23.7
Stock-based compensation expense	**19,400**	**0.2**	38,658	0.4	53,251	0.5
Interest expense	**2,066**	**–**	1,804	–	1,093	–
Earnings (loss) from continuing operations before income taxes	**95,789**	**0.9**	(1,240)	–	(5,490)	(0.1)
Income tax provision (benefit)	**35,878**	**0.3**	(453)	–	(181)	–
NET EARNINGS (LOSS) FROM CONTINUING OPERATIONS	**59,911**	**0.6**	(787)	–	(5,309)	(0.1)
NET EARNINGS (LOSS) FROM DISCONTINUED OPERATIONS	**1,747**	**–**	(88,482)	(0.9)	87,572	0.9
NET EARNINGS (LOSS)	**$ 61,658**	**0.6**	$ (89,269)	(0.9)	$ 82,263	0.8
Net earnings (loss) from discontinued operations attributed to:						
Circuit City common stock	**$ 1,747**		$ (88,482)		$ 65,264	
CarMax Group common stock	**$ –**		$ –		$ 22,308	
Weighted average common shares:						
Circuit City:						
Basic	**193,466**		205,865		207,217	
Diluted	**196,227**		205,865		207,217	
CarMax Group:						
Basic	**–**		–		37,023	
Diluted	**–**		–		38,646	
NET EARNINGS (LOSS) PER SHARE:						
Basic:						
Continuing operations	**$ 0.31**		$ –		$ (0.03)	
Discontinued operations attributed to Circuit City common stock	**0.01**		(0.43)		0.31	
	$ 0.32		$ (0.43)		$ 0.29	
Discontinued operations attributed to CarMax Group common stock	**$ –**		$ –		$ 0.60	
Diluted:						
Continuing operations	**$ 0.31**		$ –		$ (0.03)	
Discontinued operations attributed to Circuit City common stock	**0.01**		(0.43)		0.31	
	$ 0.31		$ (0.43)		$ 0.29	
Discontinued operations attributed to CarMax Group common stock	**$ –**		$ –		$ 0.58	

See accompanying notes to consolidated financial statements.

CONSOLIDATED BALANCE SHEETS

(Amounts in thousands except share data)	At February 28 or 29 2005	2004
ASSETS		
CURRENT ASSETS:		
Cash and cash equivalents	**$ 879,660**	$ 783,471
Short-term investments	**125,325**	–
Accounts receivable, net of allowance for doubtful accounts of $120 and $547	**172,995**	170,568
Retained interests in securitized receivables	**–**	425,678
Merchandise inventory	**1,459,520**	1,517,256
Deferred income taxes	**29,518**	–
Prepaid expenses and other current assets	**18,697**	22,088
TOTAL CURRENT ASSETS	**2,685,715**	2,919,061
Property and equipment, net	**738,802**	677,107
Deferred income taxes	**73,558**	88,146
Goodwill	**215,884**	–
Other intangible assets	**31,331**	–
Other assets	**44,092**	46,212
TOTAL ASSETS	**$3,789,382**	$3,730,526
LIABILITIES AND STOCKHOLDERS' EQUITY		
CURRENT LIABILITIES:		
Accounts payable	**$ 961,718**	$ 833,825
Accrued expenses and other current liabilities	**228,966**	149,605
Accrued income taxes	**72,274**	71,163
Deferred income taxes	**–**	79,422
Current installments of long-term debt	**888**	1,115
Liabilities of discontinued operations	**–**	3,068
TOTAL CURRENT LIABILITIES	**1,263,846**	1,138,198
Long-term debt, excluding current installments	**11,522**	22,691
Accrued straight-line rent and deferred rent credits	**230,426**	206,784
Accrued lease termination costs	**104,234**	75,722
Other liabilities	**91,920**	63,170
TOTAL LIABILITIES	**1,701,948**	1,506,565
STOCKHOLDERS' EQUITY:		
Common stock, $0.50 par value; 525,000,000 shares authorized; 188,150,383 shares issued and outstanding (203,899,395 in 2004)	**94,075**	101,950
Capital in excess of par value	**721,038**	922,600
Retained earnings	**1,247,221**	1,199,411
Accumulated other comprehensive income	**25,100**	–
TOTAL STOCKHOLDERS' EQUITY	**2,087,434**	2,223,961
Commitments and contingent liabilities [NOTES 12, 13 AND 16]		
TOTAL LIABILITIES AND STOCKHOLDERS' EQUITY	**$3,789,382**	$3,730,526

See accompanying notes to consolidated financial statements.

CONSOLIDATED STATEMENTS OF CASH FLOWS

(Amounts in thousands)	Years Ended February 28 or 29 2005	2004	2003
OPERATING ACTIVITIES:			
Net earnings (loss)	**$ 61,658**	$ (89,269)	$ 82,263
Adjustments to reconcile net earnings (loss) to net cash provided by (used in) operating activities of continuing operations:			
Net (earnings) loss from discontinued operations	**(1,747)**	88,482	(87,572)
Depreciation and amortization	**154,788**	197,607	159,800
Stock option expense	**18,739**	24,184	30,823
Amortization of restricted stock awards	**(434)**	13,395	20,828
(Gain) loss on dispositions of property and equipment	**(206)**	7,500	15,659
Provision for deferred income taxes	**(116,455)**	(35,618)	(18,664)
Changes in operating assets and liabilities:			
(Increase) decrease in accounts receivable, net	**(65,112)**	(30,183)	6,229
Decrease (increase) in retained interests in securitized receivables	**32,867**	(186,537)	(92,888)
Decrease (increase) in merchandise inventory	**159,278**	(107,520)	(175,493)
Decrease (increase) in prepaid expenses and other current assets	**7,148**	(3,923)	21,081
Decrease (increase) in other assets	**3,925**	12,553	(26,181)
Increase (decrease) in accounts payable	**101,991**	(85,727)	(58,041)
Increase (decrease) in accrued expenses and other current liabilities, and accrued income taxes	**36,008**	50,577	(48,069)
Increase in other long-term liabilities	**63,549**	18,966	7,116
NET CASH PROVIDED BY (USED IN) OPERATING ACTIVITIES OF CONTINUING OPERATIONS	**455,879**	(125,513)	(163,109)
INVESTING ACTIVITIES:			
Proceeds from the sale of the private-label operation	**475,857**	–	–
Acquisitions, net of cash acquired of $30,615	**(268,774)**	–	–
Purchases of property and equipment	**(269,166)**	(175,769)	(150,757)
Proceeds from sales of property and equipment	**106,369**	40,427	59,888
Purchases of investment securities	**(125,325)**	–	–
NET CASH USED IN INVESTING ACTIVITIES OF CONTINUING OPERATIONS	**(81,039)**	(135,342)	(90,869)
FINANCING ACTIVITIES:			
Payments on short-term debt	**(1,853)**	–	(397)
Principal payments on long-term debt	**(28,008)**	(1,458)	(24,865)
Repurchases of common stock	**(259,832)**	(84,353)	–
Issuances of Circuit City common stock, net	**27,156**	11,391	8,901
Issuances of CarMax Group common stock, net	–	–	298
Dividends paid	**(13,848)**	(14,660)	(14,687)
NET CASH USED IN FINANCING ACTIVITIES OF CONTINUING OPERATIONS	**(276,385)**	(89,080)	(30,750)
CASH (USED IN) PROVIDED BY DISCONTINUED OPERATIONS:			
BANKCARD OPERATION	**(4,282)**	248,736	(94,533)
CARMAX OPERATION	–	–	26,185
DIVX OPERATION	–	–	(10,500)
EFFECT OF EXCHANGE RATE CHANGES ON CASH	**2,016**	–	–
Increase (decrease) in cash and cash equivalents	**96,189**	(101,199)	(363,576)
Cash and cash equivalents at beginning of year	**783,471**	884,670	1,248,246
CASH AND CASH EQUIVALENTS AT END OF YEAR	**$ 879,660**	$ 783,471	$ 884,670

See accompanying notes to consolidated financial statements.

CONSOLIDATED STATEMENTS OF STOCKHOLDERS' EQUITY AND COMPREHENSIVE INCOME

(Amounts in thousands except per share data)	Shares Outstanding Circuit City	Shares Outstanding CarMax Group	Common Stock Circuit City	Common Stock CarMax Group	Capital In Excess of Par Value	Retained Earnings	Accumulated Other Comprehensive Income	Total
BALANCE AT FEBRUARY 28, 2002	208,823	36,851	$104,411	$ 18,426	$893,537	$1,744,129	$ —	$2,760,503
Net earnings and comprehensive income	—	—	—	—	—	82,263	—	82,263
Compensation for stock options	—	—	—	—	34,637	—	—	34,637
Exercise of common stock options	311	246	156	123	5,035	—	—	5,314
Shares issued under employee stock purchase plans	457	—	229	—	7,400	—	—	7,629
Shares issued under stock incentive plans	843	—	421	—	17,207	—	—	17,628
Tax effect from stock issued	—	—	—	—	5,986	—	—	5,986
Cancellation of restricted stock	(479)	(8)	(240)	(4)	(8,081)	—	—	(8,325)
Unearned compensation restricted stock	—	—	—	—	9,830	—	—	9,830
Cash dividends — common stock ($0.07 per share)	—	—	—	—	—	(14,687)	—	(14,687)
Distribution of CarMax, Inc. common stock to stockholders	—	(37,089)	—	(18,545)	—	(536,765)	—	(555,310)
Special dividend from CarMax	—	—	—	—	—	28,400	—	28,400
BALANCE AT FEBRUARY 28, 2003	209,955	—	104,977	—	965,551	1,303,340	—	2,373,868
Net loss and comprehensive loss	—	—	—	—	—	(89,269)	—	(89,269)
Repurchases of common stock	(9,266)	—	(4,633)	—	(79,720)	—	—	(84,353)
Compensation for stock options	—	—	—	—	24,184	—	—	24,184
Exercise of common stock options	1,369	—	685	—	11,843	—	—	12,528
Shares issued under stock incentive plans	2,546	—	1,273	—	19,312	—	—	20,585
Tax effect from stock issued	—	—	—	—	(10,595)	—	—	(10,595)
Cancellation of restricted stock	(705)	—	(352)	—	(10,074)	—	—	(10,426)
Unearned compensation restricted stock	—	—	—	—	2,099	—	—	2,099
Cash dividends — common stock ($0.07 per share)	—	—	—	—	—	(14,660)	—	(14,660)
BALANCE AT FEBRUARY 29, 2004	203,899	—	101,950	—	922,600	1,199,411	—	2,223,961
Comprehensive income:								
Net earnings	—	—	—	—	—	61,658	—	61,658
Other comprehensive income, net of taxes:								
Foreign currency translation adjustment (net of deferred taxes of $13,707)	—	—	—	—	—	—	25,100	25,100
Comprehensive income								86,758
Repurchases of common stock	(19,163)	—	(9,582)	—	(250,250)	—	—	(259,832)
Compensation for stock options	—	—	—	—	18,739	—	—	18,739
Exercise of common stock options	3,489	—	1,745	—	26,761	—	—	28,506
Shares issued under stock incentive plans	723	—	361	—	7,393	—	—	7,754
Tax effect from stock issued	—	—	—	—	(1,564)	—	—	(1,564)
Cancellation of restricted stock	(798)	—	(399)	—	(6,378)	—	—	(6,777)
Shares issued in acquisition of InterTAN, Inc.	—	—	—	—	6,498	—	—	6,498
Unearned compensation restricted stock	—	—	—	—	(2,761)	—	—	(2,761)
Cash dividends — common stock ($0.07 per share)	—	—	—	—	—	(13,848)	—	(13,848)
BALANCE AT FEBRUARY 28, 2005	188,150	—	$ 94,075	$ —	$721,038	$1,247,221	$25,100	$2,087,434

See accompanying notes to consolidated financial statements.

NOTES TO CONSOLIDATED FINANCIAL STATEMENTS

1. BASIS OF PRESENTATION

Circuit City Stores, Inc. is a leading specialty retailer of consumer electronics, home office products, entertainment software and related services. The company has two reportable segments: its domestic segment and its international segment. The domestic segment is primarily engaged in the business of selling brand-name consumer electronics, personal computers, entertainment software and services in Circuit City Superstores and mall-based stores in the United States and via the Web at www.circuitcity.com. At February 28, 2005, the company's domestic segment operated 612 Superstores and five mall-based stores in 158 U.S. media markets. The international segment is comprised of the operations of InterTAN, Inc. On May 12, 2004, the company acquired a controlling interest in InterTAN, Inc. and on May 19, 2004, completed its acquisition of 100 percent of the common stock of InterTAN for cash consideration of $259.3 million, which includes transaction costs and is net of cash acquired of $30.6 million. In addition to giving Circuit City a greater product-sourcing capability and the ability to accelerate the offering of private-label merchandise to its customers, the acquisition of InterTAN gives the company its first presence in the Canadian market. InterTAN is a leading consumer electronics retailer of both private-label and brand-name products with headquarters in Barrie, Ontario, Canada. InterTAN operates through retail stores and dealer outlets in Canada under the trade names RadioShack®, Rogers Plus® and Battery Plus®. At February 28, 2005, the international segment conducted business through 966 retail stores and dealer outlets, which consisted of 521 RadioShack® stores, 331 dealer outlets, 88 Rogers Plus® stores and 26 Battery Plus® stores. See Note 3 for additional discussion of the acquisition.

On May 25, 2004, the company completed the sale of its private-label finance operation, comprised of its private-label and co-branded Visa credit card programs, to Chase Card Services, formerly Bank One Corporation. Results from the private-label finance operation, including transition and transaction costs of approximately $6 million related to the sale of the operation, are included in finance income. The company also entered into a Consumer Credit Card Program Agreement under which Chase Card Services is offering private-label and co-branded credit cards to new and existing customers. The company is compensated under the program agreement primarily based on the number of new accounts opened less promotional financing costs that exceed a negotiated base amount. The earnings contribution from the program agreement is included in net sales and operating revenues in the consolidated statement of operations.

On November 18, 2003, the company completed the sale of its bankcard finance operation, which included Visa and MasterCard credit card receivables and related cash reserves. Results from the bankcard finance operation are presented as results from discontinued operations. See Note 17(A) for additional discussion concerning the sale of the bankcard finance operation.

From February 7, 1997, to October 1, 2002, the common stock of Circuit City Stores, Inc. consisted of two common stock series that were intended to reflect the performance of the company's two businesses. The Circuit City Group common stock was intended to reflect the performance of the Circuit City consumer electronics stores and related operations, as well as the shares of CarMax Group common stock reserved for the Circuit City Group or for issuance to holders of Circuit City Group common stock. The CarMax Group common stock was intended to reflect the performance of the CarMax auto superstores and related operations.

Effective October 1, 2002, the CarMax auto superstore business was separated from the Circuit City consumer electronics business through a tax-free transaction in which CarMax, Inc., formerly a wholly owned subsidiary of Circuit City Stores, Inc., became an independent, separately traded public company. Following the separation, the Circuit City Group common stock was renamed Circuit City common stock. CarMax results are presented as results from discontinued operations. See Note 17(B) for additional discussion of the separation.

The consolidated financial statements of the company conform to U.S. generally accepted accounting principles. Certain prior year amounts have been reclassified to conform to the current presentation. The reclassifications had no impact on results of operations, financial condition or cash flows.

During the fourth quarter of fiscal 2005, the company revised its accounting practices associated with leases, primarily related to landlord reimbursements for construction by the company on leased property. To the extent that landlord reimbursements exceed structural costs of a new store, the excess of funding over cost is classified as a long-term liability. Shortfalls in funding result in capital expenditures for structural costs in excess of reimbursements from landlords and the excess is classified as a long-term asset, unless the shortfall is substantial. In cases of substantial under-funding, the reimbursement is not used to offset capital expenditures; instead the entire amount is classified as a long-term liability.

Results for fiscal 2005 include an expense of $6.5 million for the cumulative impact of the revision to the company's lease accounting practices. The accounting revision also affected the historical balance sheets. For fiscal 2005, the impact to property and equipment was an increase of $113.0 million, the impact to other assets was an increase of $15.1 million, the impact to deferred income taxes was an increase of $2.4 million, the impact to accrued straight-line rent and deferred rent credits was an increase of $134.6 million and the impact to retained earnings was a decrease of $4.2 million. For 2004, the impact to property and equipment was an increase of $91.2 million, the impact to other assets was an increase of $17.1 million and the impact to accrued straight-line rent and deferred rent credits was an increase of $108.3 million.

During the fourth quarter of fiscal 2005, the company reclassified revenues, costs and expenses relating primarily to mobile audio installations for the domestic segment. These items, which were previously presented on a net basis as an offset to selling, general and administrative expenses, are now presented on a gross basis. The impact on the consolidated statement of operations for fiscal 2004 is an increase to revenues of $111.6 million, or 1 percent, offset by increases to cost of sales of $54.9 million, or 1 percent, and selling, general and administrative expenses of $56.7 million, or 3 percent. The impact on the consolidated statement of operations for fiscal 2003 is an increase to revenues of $101.3 million, or 1 percent, offset by increases to cost of sales of $44.8 million, or 1 percent, and selling, general and administrative expenses of $56.5 million, or 2 percent.

2. SUMMARY OF SIGNIFICANT ACCOUNTING POLICIES

Principles of Consolidation: The consolidated financial statements include the accounts of the company and its wholly owned subsidiaries. All significant intercompany balances and transactions have been eliminated in consolidation.

Use of Estimates: The preparation of financial statements in conformity with U.S. generally accepted accounting principles requires management to make estimates and assumptions that affect the reported amounts of assets, liabilities, revenues and expenses and the disclosure of contingent assets and liabilities. Actual results may differ from those estimates.

Revenue Recognition: The company recognizes revenue when the earnings process is complete, generally at either the time of sale to a customer or upon delivery to a customer. The company sells gift cards and records related deferred revenue at the time of sale. The domestic segment sells extended warranty contracts on behalf of unrelated third parties. The contracts extend beyond the normal manufacturer's warranty period, usually with terms, including the manufacturer's warranty period, from 12 to 60 months. Because the third parties are the primary obligors under these contracts, commission revenue for the unrelated-third-party extended warranty plans is recognized at the time of sale. For the international segment, the company is the primary obligor for its extended warranty programs. Accordingly, extended warranty revenue is deferred at point of sale and recognized as revenue over the life of the contract.

Cost of Sales, Buying and Warehousing: Cost of sales, buying and warehousing includes the cost of the merchandise sold or services performed, the cost of transportation of merchandise from vendors to the company's stores, the operating costs of the company's service and distribution centers, as well as the company's merchandising costs.

Vendor Allowances: The company receives cash consideration from vendors through a variety of programs and arrangements, including cooperative advertising and vendor allowances. The majority of vendor allowances are recognized as a reduction to cost of sales, buying and warehousing. Cash consideration received as part of cooperative advertising programs that represents a reimbursement of specific, incremental, identifiable direct costs incurred by the company to advertise the vendors' products is reported as a reduction to advertising expense in the period in which the advertising costs are incurred.

Interest Income: Interest income recorded as a reduction to selling, general and administrative expenses was $14.4 million for the fiscal year ended February 28, 2005, $6.6 million for the fiscal year ended February 29, 2004, and $7.9 million for the fiscal year ended February 28, 2003.

Store Opening and Location Closing Expenses: Non-capital expenditures relating to store openings, including organization and pre-opening costs, are expensed as incurred. When the company commits to a plan to close or relocate a store, estimates of the depreciable lives of fixtures, equipment and leasehold improvements to be abandoned are revised to reflect the use of the assets over their shortened useful lives. At a location's cease-use date, estimated unrecoverable costs are charged to selling, general and administrative expenses. These costs are included in accrued lease termination costs on the consolidated balance sheets and may include a provision for the present value of future lease obligations, less contractual or estimated sublease income.

Advertising Expenses: Advertising costs are expensed as incurred and are included in selling, general and administrative expenses on the consolidated statements of operations. Advertising expense was $361.3 million in fiscal 2005, $319.6 million in fiscal 2004 and $345.1 million in fiscal 2003.

Stock-Based Compensation: The company sponsors various stock incentive plans. Effective December 1, 2003, the company adopted the fair value-based method of accounting for stock-based compensation. The adoption was applied using the retroactive restatement method and all periods have been retroactively restated to reflect the compensation cost that would have been recognized had the fair value-based method been applied to all awards granted to employees in fiscal years beginning after December 15, 1994. Accordingly, the company values stock options using the Black-Scholes option valuation model and recognizes expense over the options' vesting period. For restricted stock, the market value at the grant date is recorded as unearned compensation in stockholders' equity and expensed over the restriction periods.

Certain restricted stock awards vest based upon the company achieving operating profit margin targets. The expense related to the performance-based awards is recognized based on the likelihood of management achieving the performance targets.

Net Earnings Per Share: Basic net earnings per share is computed using the weighted average number of shares of common stock outstanding. Diluted net earnings per share is computed using the weighted average common and potentially dilutive common equivalent shares outstanding.

For fiscal 2003, the shares of CarMax Group common stock were weighted over the months during which CarMax was a wholly owned subsidiary of the company. CarMax became an independent, separately traded public company on October 1, 2002.

Foreign Currency Translation: The local currency of InterTAN, the Canadian dollar, is its functional currency. For reporting purposes, InterTAN's assets and liabilities are translated into U.S. dollars using the exchange rates in effect at the balance sheet date. Income and expense items are translated using monthly average exchange rates. The effects of exchange rate changes on the translation of the net assets of InterTAN are included as a component of stockholders' equity in accumulated other comprehensive income. Gains and losses from foreign currency transactions are included in selling, general and administrative expenses in the consolidated statements of operations.

Fair Value of Financial Instruments: The carrying values of the company's cash and cash equivalents, short-term investments, accounts receivable, accounts payable and long-term debt approximate fair value. Retained interests in securitized receivables and derivative financial instruments are recorded on the consolidated balance sheets at fair value.

Cash and Cash Equivalents: Cash and cash equivalents consist of cash on hand and highly liquid investments with original maturities of three months or less. Cash equivalents include investments in highly liquid debt securities with original maturities of three months or less of $836.0 million at February 28, 2005, and $699.6 million at February 29, 2004. All cash and cash equivalents were available for general corporate purposes at February 28, 2005. Cash and cash equivalents held by the company's regulated subsidiaries and not available for general corporate purposes were $58.3 million at February 29, 2004.

Short-Term Investments: As part of its cash management program, the company from time to time maintains a portfolio of marketable investment securities. The securities, which have an investment grade and a term to earliest maturity of three to 12 months, include $100.3 million in treasury notes and $25.0 million in commercial paper and are classified as held-to-maturity securities. These securities are carried at cost, which approximates fair value.

Securitizations: Prior to the sale of the private-label finance operation, the company entered into securitization transactions to finance credit card receivables originated by its finance operation. These transactions were accounted for as sales in accordance with SFAS No. 140, "Accounting for Transfers and Servicing of Financial Assets and Extinguishment of Liabilities." At February 29, 2004, retained interests in securitized receivables were carried at fair value as determined by the estimated net proceeds from the planned sale of the company's private-label finance operation. The changes in fair value of retained interests are included in finance income on the consolidated statements of operations. See Note 6 for additional discussion of securitizations.

Derivative Financial Instruments: Prior to the sale of the private-label finance operation, the company entered into interest rate cap agreements in connection with its securitization transactions. The company recognized all derivative instruments as either assets or liabilities on the consolidated balance sheets at fair value. Fair value estimates of the company's derivative instruments were based on quoted market prices.

Merchandise Inventory: Inventory is comprised of finished goods held for sale and is stated at the lower of cost or market. Cost is determined by the average cost method. The company estimates the realizable value of inventory based on assumptions about forecasted consumer demand, market conditions and obsolescence. If the estimated realizable value is less than cost, the inventory value is reduced to its estimated realizable value. If estimates regarding consumer demand and market conditions are inaccurate or unexpected changes in technology affect demand, the company could be exposed to losses in excess of amounts recorded.

Property and Equipment: Property and equipment is stated at cost less accumulated depreciation and amortization. Depreciation and amortization are calculated using the straight-line method over the assets' estimated useful lives. Property held under capital lease is stated at the lower of the present value of the future minimum lease payments at the inception of the lease or market value and is amortized on a straight-line basis over the lease term or the estimated useful life of the asset, whichever is shorter. The company capitalizes external direct costs of materials and services used in the development of internal-use software and payroll and payroll-related costs for employees directly involved in the development of internal-use software. Amounts capitalized are included in furniture, fixtures and equipment and are amortized on a straight-line basis over a period of three years to five years.

Impairment or Disposal of Long-Lived Assets: The company reviews long-lived assets for impairment when circumstances indicate the carrying amount of an asset may not be recoverable. Impairment is recognized when the sum of undiscounted estimated future cash flows expected to result from the use of the asset is less than the asset's carrying value. The impairment loss recognized represents the difference between the asset's carrying value and its estimated fair value.

Deferred Income Taxes: Deferred income taxes reflect the impact of temporary differences between the amounts of assets and liabilities recognized for financial reporting purposes and the amounts recognized for income tax purposes, measured by applying currently enacted tax laws. The company recognizes a deferred tax asset if it is more likely than not that the company will realize a benefit from that deferred tax asset.

Goodwill and Other Intangible Assets: The excess of the purchase price over the fair value of identifiable net assets of acquired companies is allocated to goodwill. Goodwill is evaluated for impairment on an annual basis, during the second quarter of each fiscal year, or more frequently if an event or circumstance indicates that the asset may be impaired. Through the impairment test, goodwill, other intangible assets, and tangible assets and liabilities are divided among reporting units. If the fair value of those reporting units is less than the carrying value, then the implied fair value of the goodwill of the reporting unit must be compared to the carrying value of that goodwill. If the fair value of the goodwill is less than the carrying value, goodwill is deemed to be impaired and an impairment loss, equal to the excess of the carrying value over the fair value, must be recorded. The identifiable intangible assets are amortized on a straight-line basis over their estimated useful lives.

Accrued Straight-Line Rent: Most of the company's leases include fixed-dollar rental commitments, with many containing rent escalations based on the lesser of a fixed amount or a multiple of the change in the Consumer Price Index. In accordance with Statement of Financial Accounting Standards No. 13, "Accounting for Leases," as amended by SFAS No. 29, "Determining Contingent Rentals," and Financial Accounting Standards Board Technical Bulletin 85-3, "Accounting for Operating Leases with Scheduled Rent Increases," the company recognizes rental expense for minimum lease payments from operating leases on a straight-line basis. Accrued straight-line rent is included in accrued straight-line rent and deferred rent credits on the consolidated balance sheets.

Landlord Reimbursements: The company conducts a substantial portion of its business in leased properties. The company constructs stores on both owned and leased land and may receive reimbursement from the landlord for the cost of the structure. These transactions are evaluated for sale-leaseback accounting and in cases where substantial funding is received, the transaction qualifies for sale-leaseback accounting. Any gain or loss from the transaction is deferred and amortized on a straight-line basis over the base term of the lease.

In cases where reimbursement from the landlord results in substantial under-funding of costs incurred for the construction of the building, the company is deemed to have continuing involvement and the transaction does not qualify for sale-leaseback accounting. Instead, the landlord reimbursement is considered a financing and included in deferred rent credits on the consolidated balance sheets. The financing is amortized using the interest method over the base term of the lease.

In instances where the company leases an existing structure, reimbursements from the landlord for tenant improvements are classified as incentives in deferred rent credits on the consolidated balance sheets. These deferred rent credits are amortized on a straight-line basis over the base term of the lease.

Accumulated Other Comprehensive Income: Accumulated other comprehensive income is comprised of foreign currency translation adjustments and is recorded net of deferred income taxes directly as a component of stockholders' equity.

Risks and Uncertainties: The company is a leading specialty retailer of brand-name consumer electronics, personal computers and entertainment software. The diversity of the company's products, customers, suppliers and geographic operations reduces the risk that a severe impact will occur in the near term as a result of changes in its customer base, competition, sources of supply or markets.

The international segment has 109 employees, or approximately 3 percent of its employees, who are represented by a union. These 109 employees are located in InterTAN's distribution center in Barrie, Ontario, Canada. In April 2003, the terms of a three-year collective bargaining agreement were ratified with these employees.

3. ACQUISITIONS

(A) InterTAN, Inc.: On May 12, 2004, the company acquired a controlling interest in InterTAN, Inc. and on May 19, 2004, completed its acquisition of 100 percent of the common stock of InterTAN for cash consideration of $259.3 million, which includes transaction costs and is net of cash acquired of $30.6 million. This acquisition was accounted for using the purchase method. Accordingly, the company recorded the net assets at their estimated fair values and included operating results in the consolidated financial statements since May 12, 2004. The company allocated the purchase price to the acquired assets and liabilities using available information. The purchase price allocation includes goodwill of $185.4 million and identifiable intangible assets of $28.0 million. Goodwill is not deductible for tax purposes. The identifiable intangible assets consist of contract-based intangibles and are amortized on a straight-line basis over their estimated useful lives, which range from 4.5 years to 20 years. See Note 9 and Note 19 for additional discussion.

Selected unaudited pro forma financial information assuming the acquisition had been consummated at the beginning of fiscal 2004 is as follows:

	(Unaudited) Years Ended February 28 or 29	
	2005	2004
(Amounts in millions except per share data)	Pro Forma	Pro Forma
Net sales and operating revenues	$10,551.7	$10,321.0
Net earnings from continuing operations	$ 60.2	$ 5.5
Net earnings per share from continuing operations	$ 0.31	$ 0.03

After Circuit City's March 31, 2004, announcement of its agreement to acquire InterTAN, RadioShack Corporation asserted early termination of its licensing and other agreements with InterTAN. On April 5, 2004, RadioShack filed suit against InterTAN, and amended that suit on April 27, 2004 (the "RadioShack litigation"). InterTAN disputes the termination scenarios alleged by RadioShack and is vigorously defending against those claims. InterTAN also has filed claims for disparagement and unfair business practices against RadioShack. The parties argued a RadioShack motion for partial summary judgment on February 3, 2005. On March 24, 2005, the court issued an order on that motion stating that the three agreements were terminated no later than December 31, 2004. If that ruling stands, there would be a six-month wind down period under the license agreement until June 30, 2005.

Circuit City believes that RadioShack is not entitled to early termination of the agreements and that InterTAN has substantial defenses to the RadioShack claims. Circuit City and InterTAN intend to vigorously defend the claims in the RadioShack litigation. Circuit City believes that this litigation will not have a material adverse effect on the company's financial condition or results of operations.

(B) MusicNow, Inc.: On April 2, 2004, the company completed its acquisition of MusicNow, Inc., a provider of licensed digital media content, for a purchase price of $6.5 million. MusicNow provides customers with approximately one million music titles for download through its Web site, www.musicnow.com.

4. FINANCE INCOME

Finance income includes the results from the company's private-label finance operation, including transition and transaction costs of approximately $6 million related to the sale of the operation to Chase Card Services, through May 25, 2004, the date the company completed the sale.

Components of pretax finance income were as follows:

	Years Ended February 28 or 29		
(Amounts in millions)	2005	2004	2003
Securitization income	$28.1	$120.9	$107.3
Less: Payroll and fringe benefits expenses	7.6	29.5	30.8
Other direct expenses	14.9	58.7	49.2
Finance income	$ 5.6	$ 32.7	$ 27.3

Securitization income primarily is comprised of the gain on the sale of receivables generated by the company's private-label finance operation, income from the retained interests in the credit card receivables and income related to servicing the receivables, as well as the impact of increases or decreases in the fair value of the retained interests. Securitization income is reduced by payroll, fringe benefits and other costs directly associated with the management and securitization of the private-label receivables.

5. NET EARNINGS (LOSS) PER SHARE

The following table presents a reconciliation of the denominators used in the net earnings (loss) per share calculations.

(Amounts in thousands)	Years Ended February 28 or 29 2005	2004	2003
Circuit City:			
Weighted average common shares	193,466	205,865	207,217
Dilutive potential common shares:			
Options	2,239	–	–
Restricted stock	522	–	–
Weighted average common shares and dilutive potential common shares	196,227	205,865	207,217
CarMax Group:			
Weighted average common shares	–	–	37,023
Dilutive potential common shares:			
Options	–	–	1,613
Restricted stock	–	–	10
Weighted average common shares and dilutive potential common shares	–	–	38,646

The fiscal 2005 computation of dilutive potential common shares excluded certain options to purchase shares of Circuit City common stock because the exercise prices were greater than the average market price of the common shares and, therefore, the effect would be anti-dilutive. For fiscal 2004 and fiscal 2003, no options or restricted stock were included in the calculation of Circuit City's diluted net loss per share because the company reported a loss from continuing operations. Shares excluded were as follows:

(Shares in millions)	Years Ended February 28 or 29 2005	2004	2003
Options to purchase Circuit City common stock	6.1	17.8	17.6
Restricted stock	–	1.6	2.8

For fiscal 2003, the shares of CarMax Group common stock were weighted over the months during which CarMax was a wholly owned subsidiary of Circuit City Stores, Inc. Options to purchase 1.0 million shares of CarMax Group common stock were outstanding at the separation date and not included in the calculation of diluted net earnings per share at the end of fiscal 2003.

6. SECURITIZATIONS

Prior to the sale of its private-label finance operation on May 25, 2004, the company entered into securitization transactions to finance its private-label and co-branded Visa credit card receivables, collectively referred to as private-label receivables, originated by its finance operation. The company used a special purpose subsidiary to facilitate these securitization transactions in accordance with the isolation provisions of SFAS No. 140. The finance operation sold the private-label receivables to the special purpose subsidiary, which, in turn, transferred these receivables to a securitization master trust. At the time of these sales, the company recognized gains or losses as a component of finance income. See Note 4 for discussion of finance income.

The company funded its Mastercard and non-co-branded Visa credit card receivables through a similar master trust program prior to the sale of its bankcard finance operation to FleetBoston Financial in November 2003. See Note 17(A) for discussion of the discontinued bankcard operation.

The master trusts periodically issued securities backed by the credit card receivables. The master trusts issued multiple series of term asset-backed securities each having a fixed initial principal amount and multiple series of variable funding asset-backed securities each having a variable principal amount. The finance operations continued to service the securitized receivables for an annual fee approximating 2 percent of the outstanding principal balance of the securitized receivables. The servicing fees specified in the securitization agreements adequately compensated the finance operations for servicing the securitized receivables. Accordingly, no servicing asset or liability was recorded.

Circuit City retained the right to receive the excess of the finance charges and fees generated by the securitized receivables over the interest paid to investors, servicing costs and credit losses. The company also held various subordinated asset-backed securities that served as credit enhancement for the asset-backed securities held by third-party investors.

The following table summarizes cash flows received from and paid to the securitization trusts.

(Amounts in millions)	Years Ended February 29 or 28 2004	2003
Proceeds from new securitizations	$ 500.6	$ 901.0
Proceeds from collections reinvested in previous credit card securitizations	$1,785.9	$1,157.3
Servicing fees received	$ 30.3	$ 24.7
Other cash flows received on retained interests*	$ 131.9	$ 73.7

*This amount represents cash flows received from retained interests other than servicing fees.

Gains on sales of receivables sold to the securitization trusts were $47.7 million for fiscal 2004 and $67.8 million for fiscal 2003.

At February 29, 2004, the fair value of the retained interests in securitized private-label receivables was $425.7 million and was determined based on the estimated net proceeds from the planned sale of the company's private-label finance operation.

7. FINANCIAL DERIVATIVES

Prior to the sale of the private-label and bankcard finance operations, the company entered into interest rate cap agreements in connection with its receivable securitization transactions. The company has no obligations under these derivatives following the sale of the private-label operation. The company did not purchase or sell any interest rate caps in fiscal 2005 or 2004. The total notional amount of interest rate caps outstanding was $280.5 million at February 29, 2004. Interest rate caps purchased by the company are included in net accounts receivable on the consolidated balance sheets and had a fair value of $2.7 million at February 29, 2004. Interest rate caps written by the company are included in accounts payable on the consolidated balance sheets and had a fair value of $2.7 million at February 29, 2004. Fair value was determined from quoted market prices.

8. PROPERTY AND EQUIPMENT

Property and equipment, stated at cost, is summarized as follows:

(Amounts in millions)	At February 28 or 29 2005	2004
Land	$ 28.8	$ 15.9
Buildings (up to 25 years)	285.7	284.7
Construction in progress	68.4	15.3
Furniture, fixtures and equipment (1 to 8 years)	841.3	815.1
Leasehold improvements (up to 15 years)	612.2	607.0
Capital leases, primarily buildings (19 to 27 years)	6.5	3.7
	1,842.9	1,741.7
Less accumulated depreciation and amortization	1,104.1	1,064.6
Property and equipment, net	$ 738.8	$ 677.1

When the company commits to a plan to abandon a long-lived asset before the end of its previously estimated useful life, the company revises depreciation estimates. For fiscal 2005, accumulated depreciation and amortization includes $0.8 million of accelerated depreciation for assets expected to be disposed in fiscal 2006. For fiscal 2004, accumulated depreciation and amortization includes $1.5 million of accelerated depreciation for assets then expected to be disposed in fiscal 2005.

9. GOODWILL AND OTHER INTANGIBLE ASSETS

The changes in the carrying amount of goodwill by reportable segment for the year ended February 28, 2005, were as follows:

(Amounts in millions)	Domestic Segment	International Segment	Total
Balance at February 29, 2004	$ –	$ –	$ –
Goodwill resulting from acquisitions	3.1	188.4	191.5
Increase due to foreign currency translation	–	24.4	24.4
Balance at February 28, 2005	$3.1	$212.8	$215.9

Acquired other intangible assets at February 28, 2005, were as follows:

	At February 28, 2005		
(Dollar amounts in millions)	Gross Carrying Value	Weighted Average Amortization Period (in years)	Accumulated Amortization
Dealer-relationship contracts	$14.6	20.0	$0.6
Vendor contract	11.2	10.0	0.8
Employment agreements	5.6	4.5	0.9
Other	2.9	2.9	0.7
Total	$34.3	12.8	$3.0

Amortization expense was $3.0 million for the year ended February 28, 2005. Estimated amortization expense for the next five fiscal years is $4.1 million in 2006, $4.1 million in 2007, $3.2 million in 2008, $2.8 million in 2009, and $1.9 million in 2010. These amortization expense estimates are subject to fluctuations in foreign currency exchange rates. See Note 3 and Note 19 for additional discussion of goodwill and other intangible assets.

10. DEBT

Long-term debt is summarized as follows:

	At February 28 or 29	
(Amounts in millions)	2005	2004
Industrial Development Revenue Bonds at various prime-based rates of interest ranging from 2.6% to 3.3% in fiscal 2004	$ –	$ 0.7
Obligations under capital leases	12.4	10.5
Other	–	12.6
Total long-term debt	12.4	23.8
Less current installments	0.9	1.1
Long-term debt, excluding current installments	$11.5	$22.7

On June 27, 2003, the company entered into a $500 million, four-year revolving credit facility secured by inventory and accounts receivable. This facility is used to support letters of credit and for short-term borrowing needs. Loans primarily bear interest at a spread over LIBOR or at prime. The facility is scheduled to mature in June 2007 and provides for a one-year extension. The maximum credit extensions, including loans and outstanding letters of credit, permitted under the credit facility on any date are determined by calculating a borrowing base that is a percentage of the company's eligible inventory and accounts receivable as of the date of the credit extension. If the remaining borrowing availability under the facility falls below $100 million, cash dividends and stock repurchases are limited to an aggregate of $75 million in any fiscal year. In addition, if the remaining borrowing availability under the facility falls below $50 million for five consecutive business days, all proceeds from the sale of inventory must be applied on a daily basis to payment of amounts owed under the facility. The facility has representations and warranties, covenants and events of default that are customary for this type of credit facility. On July 8, 2004, the credit agreement was amended to include InterTAN as a borrower. The amended credit agreement established a $400 million borrowing limit for the domestic segment and a $100 million borrowing limit for the international segment. At February 28, 2005, the company had no short-term borrowings on this facility, and outstanding letters of credit related to this facility were $56.2 million, leaving $443.8 million available for borrowing. At February 29, 2004, the company had no short-term borrowings on this facility. At February 29, 2004, outstanding letters of credit related to this facility were $37.3 million, leaving $462.7 million available for borrowing.

The Industrial Development Revenue Bonds were repaid in the second quarter of fiscal 2005.

Other debt represents the liability assumed from a variable interest entity with an aggregate principal amount totaling $12.6 million at February 29, 2004. The company leased a corporate office building under a synthetic operating lease arrangement with a variable interest entity. This arrangement was terminated and the related debt was extinguished on February 10, 2005.

The scheduled aggregate annual principal payments on long-term debt obligations for the next five fiscal years are as follows:

Fiscal Year	(Amounts in millions)
2006	$0.9
2007	$1.0
2008	$1.2
2009	$1.3
2010	$1.5

11. INCOME TAXES

The earnings (loss) from continuing operations before income taxes were as follows:

	Years Ended February 28 or 29		
(Amounts in millions)	2005	2004	2003
U. S. earnings	$57.3	$(1.2)	$(5.5)
Foreign earnings	38.5	–	–
Earnings (loss) from continuing operations before income taxes	$95.8	$(1.2)	$(5.5)

Total income taxes on earnings (loss) were allocated as follows:

	Years Ended February 28 or 29		
(Amounts in millions)	2005	2004	2003
Income tax provision (benefit) from continuing operations	$35.9	$ (0.5)	$(0.2)
Income tax provision (benefit) from discontinued operations	1.0	(49.8)	55.0
Total income tax provision (benefit)	$36.8	$(50.2)	$54.9

The components of income tax provision (benefit) on earnings (loss) from continuing operations were as follows:

	Years Ended February 28 or 29		
(Amounts in millions)	2005	2004	2003
Current			
Federal	$ 130.3	$ 33.9	$ 16.5
Foreign	14.4	–	–
State	7.7	1.2	1.9
	152.4	35.2	18.5
Deferred:			
Federal	$(112.3)	$(34.4)	$(18.2)
Foreign	(0.1)	–	–
State	(4.1)	(1.2)	(0.4)
	(116.5)	(35.6)	(18.7)
Income tax provision (benefit)	$ 35.9	$ (0.5)	$ (0.2)

The company files a consolidated federal income tax return for its U. S. operations. The company has not provided for U.S. deferred income taxes or foreign withholding taxes on pre-acquisition earnings of its foreign subsidiaries because the company deems these earnings to be permanently reinvested. If these pre-acquisition earnings were not considered permanently reinvested, an additional deferred income tax liability of $6.0 million would have been provided.

The American Jobs Creation Act of 2004 provides a temporary incentive for U. S. corporations to repatriate accumulated income earned abroad by providing an 85 percent dividend received deduction, provided certain criteria are met. The company completed its analysis of this provision and determined that it will not benefit from the dividend received deduction because it continues to believe its pre-acquisition earnings from foreign subsidiaries will remain permanently reinvested.

The effective income tax rate applicable to results from continuing operations differed from the federal statutory income tax rate as follows:

	Years Ended February 28 or 29		
	2005	2004	2003
Federal statutory income tax rate	35.0%	35.0%	35.0%
State and local income taxes, net of federal benefit	2.6	(1.1)	(17.9)
Non-deductible meals and entertainment	0.2	(28.5)	(15.5)
Non-deductible contributions	–	(3.3)	(0.8)
Resolution of prior year taxes	–	10.3	–
Taxes on foreign income that differ from the federal statutory rate	1.1	–	–
Change in value of deferred tax (liability) asset	(0.7)	2.8	(0.9)
Federal and state tax credits	(0.7)	21.3	3.4
Effective income tax rate	37.5%	36.5%	3.3%

In accordance with SFAS No. 109, "Accounting for Income Taxes," the tax effects of temporary differences that give rise to a significant portion of the deferred tax assets and liabilities from continuing operations were as follows:

	At February 28 or 29	
(Amounts in millions)	2005	2004
Deferred tax assets:		
Accrued liabilities	$ 81.7	$ 63.4
Stock-based compensation	36.6	38.1
Merchandise inventory	1.9	–
Accrued straight-line rent and deferred rent credits	84.4	74.0
Deferred revenue	7.5	–
Foreign tax credits	5.9	–
Other	1.2	2.0
Gross deferred tax assets	219.1	177.5
Valuation allowance	(5.9)	–
Total deferred tax assets	$213.2	$177.5
Deferred tax liabilities:		
Deferred revenue	–	53.0
Depreciation and amortization	81.1	54.6
Securitized receivables	–	23.0
Merchandise inventory	–	16.5
Prepaid expenses	15.3	21.7
Foreign currency translation adjustment	13.7	–
Total deferred tax liabilities	110.1	168.8
Net deferred tax asset	$103.1	$ 8.7

Deferred tax assets and liabilities were included in the balance sheets as follows:

	February 28 or 29	
(Amounts in millions)	2005	2004
Current deferred tax assets in excess of liabilities	$ 29.5	$ –
Current deferred tax liabilities in excess of assets	–	79.4
Non-current deferred tax assets in excess of liabilities	73.6	88.1
Net deferred tax asset	$103.1	$ 8.7

Deferred income taxes at February 28, 2005, include a $5.9 million deferred tax asset associated with foreign tax credits created by the international segment. Due to the uncertainty regarding the realization of this tax benefit, management has provided a full valuation allowance against the deferred tax asset.

Based on the company's historical and current pretax earnings, management believes the remaining deferred tax assets will more likely than not be realized.

12. LEASE COMMITMENTS

The company conducts a substantial portion of its business in leased premises. The company's lease obligations are based upon contractual minimum rates.

Rent expense for all operating leases on active properties and equipment is summarized as follows:

(Amounts in millions)	Years Ended February 28 or 29 2005	2004	2003
Minimum rentals	$335.9	$308.0	$314.2
Rentals based on sales volume	0.5	0.1	0.2
Total rent expense	$336.4	$308.1	$314.4

Most of the company's leases are fixed-dollar rental commitments, with many containing rent escalations based on the lesser of a fixed amount or a multiple of the change in the Consumer Price Index. Several store leases include rental commitments based on a percentage of sales volumes in excess of defined amounts. Most leases provide that the company pay taxes, maintenance, insurance and operating expenses applicable to the premises.

The initial term of most real property leases will expire within the next 20 years; however, most of the leases have options providing for additional lease terms of five to 25 years at terms similar to the initial terms.

Future minimum fixed lease obligations, including closed locations and excluding taxes, insurance and other costs payable directly by the company, as of February 28, 2005, were as follows:

(Amounts in millions) Fiscal Year	Capital Leases	Operating Lease Commitments	Operating Sublease Income
2006	$ 2.1	$ 406.6	$ 51.9
2007	2.2	404.0	48.5
2008	2.2	398.6	45.1
2009	2.2	390.2	41.6
2010	2.2	381.5	40.1
After 2010	8.4	3,096.7	335.9
Total minimum lease payments	19.4	$5,077.6	$563.1
Less amounts representing interest	7.0		
Present value of net minimum capital lease payments	$12.4		

CarMax currently operates 23 of its sales locations pursuant to leases under which the company is the primary obligor. In conjunction with the separation, the company assigned each of these operating leases to CarMax. CarMax paid a special dividend of $28.4 million to Circuit City Stores, Inc. in recognition of the company's continuing contingent liability on the leases related to these CarMax locations. At February 28, 2005, the future minimum fixed lease obligations on these 23 leases totaled $422.9 million. Amounts presented within the above table reflect the company's lease commitments on these leases and the corresponding sublease income associated with these CarMax locations.

The company constructs stores on both owned and leased land. The company may receive reimbursement from the landlord for the cost of the structure. These transactions are evaluated for sale-leaseback accounting and in cases where substantial funding is received, the transaction qualifies for sale-leaseback accounting. Any gain or loss from the transaction is deferred and included in other assets or deferred rent credits on the consolidated balance sheets and amortized on a straight-line basis over the base term of the lease. Proceeds from sale-leaseback transactions totaled $88.5 million in fiscal 2005, $38.3 million in fiscal 2004 and $52.3 million in 2003.

In cases where the landlord reimbursement results in a substantial under-funding of costs incurred for the construction of the building, the company is deemed to have continuing involvement and thus the transaction does not qualify for sale-leaseback accounting. Instead, the landlord reimbursement is considered a financing and included in deferred rent credits on the consolidated balance sheets. The financing liability is amortized using the interest method over the base term of the lease. No lease entered into in fiscal 2005, fiscal 2004 and fiscal 2003 qualified for treatment as financing. The financing liability associated with leases entered into prior to fiscal 2003, was $11.6 million at February 28, 2005, $13.9 million at February 29, 2004 and $14.1 million at February 28, 2003.

In some instances, the company leases land with an existing structure at the inception of the lease. The company may receive an incentive from the landlord for improvements to the structure. Under these circumstances, the company classifies the incentive as deferred rent credits and amortizes the incentive on a straight-line basis over the base term of the lease.

Incentives qualifying for such treatment totaled $11.0 million in fiscal 2005, $6.2 million in fiscal 2004 and $1.0 million in fiscal 2003.

Accrued lease termination costs were $141.7 million at February 28, 2005, of which $37.5 million is current and included in accrued expenses and other current liabilities and the non-current portion of $104.2 million is presented separately on the consolidated balance sheets. Accrued lease termination costs were $105.3 million at February 29, 2004, of which $29.6 million is current and included in accrued expenses and other current liabilities and the non-current portion of $75.6 million is presented separately on the consolidated balance sheets.

13. CONTINGENT LIABILITIES

In the normal course of business, the company is involved in various legal proceedings. Based upon the company's evaluation of the information presently available, management believes that the ultimate resolution of any such proceedings will not have a material adverse effect on the company's financial condition, liquidity or results of operations. See Note 3 concerning the RadioShack litigation.

14. CAPITAL STOCK

(A) Shareholder Rights Plan: In conjunction with the company's shareholder rights plan as amended and restated, preferred share purchase rights were distributed as a dividend at the rate of one right for each share of common stock. The rights are exercisable only upon the attainment of, or the commencement of a tender offer to attain, a specified ownership interest in the company by a person or group. When exercisable, each right would entitle the holder to buy one eight-hundredth of a share of Cumulative Participating Preferred Stock, Series E, $20 par value, at an exercise price of $125 per share, subject to adjustment. A total of 500,000 shares of such preferred stock, which have preferential dividend and liquidation rights, have been designated. No such shares are outstanding. In the event that an acquiring person or group acquires 15 percent or more of the company's common stock, except pursuant to a cash tender offer for all outstanding shares determined to be fair by the board of directors, or engages in certain transactions with the company after the rights become exercisable, each right would be converted into a right to purchase, for half the current market price at that time, shares of stock valued at two times the exercise price. In February 2004, the company's board of directors voted to terminate the company's shareholder rights plan effective May 1, 2005. In April 2005, the company's board of directors ordered the redemption of all outstanding preferred share purchase rights under the shareholder rights plan. The company will pay on May 15, 2005, a redemption price equal to one cent per share of the company's common stock to shareholders of record at the close of business on May 1, 2005. The preferred share purchase rights terminated effective May 1, 2005.

(B) Preferred Stock: The company has 1.0 million shares of undesignated preferred stock authorized of which no shares are outstanding.

(C) Common Stock Repurchased: In January 2003, the company's board of directors authorized the repurchase of up to $200 million of common stock. In June 2004, the board authorized a $200 million increase in its stock repurchase authorization, raising the total repurchase capacity to $400 million. In March 2005, the board authorized a $400 million increase in its stock repurchase authorization, raising the total repurchase capacity to $800 million, of which $455.8 million remained available at March 31, 2005. The company repurchased 19.2 million shares of common stock at a cost of $259.8 million during fiscal 2005. The company repurchased 9.3 million shares of common stock at a cost of $84.4 million during fiscal 2004. As of February 28, 2005, the company had repurchased 28.4 million shares of common stock at a cost of $344.2 million.

15. STOCK-BASED INCENTIVE PLANS

Under the company's stock-based incentive plans, nonqualified stock options, restricted stock, restricted stock units and other equity-based awards may be granted to management, key employees and non-employee directors. The exercise price for nonqualified options must be equal to, or greater than, the market value at the date of grant. Options generally are exercisable over a period of one year to 10 years from the date of grant. At February 28, 2005, 1.9 million shares of common stock were available for future grants of options, restricted stock or restricted stock units. The number of shares available for grant at February 29, 2004, was 4.2 million shares of common stock.

(A) Stock Options: Effective December 1, 2003, the company adopted the fair value recognition provisions of SFAS No. 123, as amended by SFAS No. 148, which requires that the company value stock options issued based upon an option pricing model and recognize this value as an expense over the period in which the options vest. The adoption of this standard was applied using the retroactive restatement method as defined in SFAS No. 148.

The Black-Scholes option valuation model was developed for use in estimating the fair value of traded options that do not have vesting restrictions and that are fully transferable. Option valuation models require the company to make highly subjective assumptions, including the expected future volatility of the stock price, expected dividend yield, risk-free interest rate and expected life of the option. Because the stock options granted by the company have characteristics that are significantly different from those of traded options, and because changes in the subjective assumptions can materially affect the fair value estimate, the existing option valuation models, including the Black-Scholes model, do not necessarily provide a reliable single measure of the fair value of the company's employee stock options.

The fair value of each option granted is estimated on the grant date using the Black-Scholes option-pricing model with the following weighted average assumptions:

	Years Ended February 28 or 29		
	2005	2004	2003
Expected dividend yield	0.6%	1.1%	0.3%
Expected stock volatility	64%	76%	70%
Risk-free interest rates	4%	3%	5%
Expected lives (in years)	4	5	5

Using these assumptions in the Black-Scholes model, the weighted average fair value of options granted was $6.63 per share in fiscal 2005, $3.58 per share in fiscal 2004 and $12.70 per share in fiscal 2003.

Compensation expense from continuing operations arising from stock option grants as determined using the Black-Scholes fair value option model was $18.7 million in fiscal 2005, $24.2 million in fiscal 2004 and $30.8 million in fiscal 2003 and is included in stock-based compensation expense on the consolidated statements of operations.

The company's stock option activity is summarized in Table 1. Table 2 summarizes information about stock options outstanding as of February 28, 2005.

TABLE 1	2005		2004		2003	
(Shares in thousands)	Shares	Weighted Average Exercise Price	Shares	Weighted Average Exercise Price	Shares	Weighted Average Exercise Price
Outstanding at beginning of year	17,829	$14.31	17,622	$15.44	11,991	$23.60
Granted	3,109	12.60	4,426	6.43	1,520	21.30
InterTAN acquisition grants	1,128	6.01	–	–	–	–
Adjustments due to CarMax separation:						
Granted	–	–	–	–	17,865	15.42
Cancelled	–	–	–	–	(11,911)	23.14
Exercised	(3,489)	8.17	(1,369)	9.15	(311)	13.06
Cancelled	(1,974)	12.24	(2,850)	11.54	(1,532)	25.60
Outstanding at end of year	16,602	$14.96	17,829	$14.31	17,622	$15.44
Options exercisable at end of year	10,627	$17.71	10,351	$17.36	9,092	$16.97

TABLE 2	Options Outstanding			Options Exercisable	
(Shares in thousands) Range of Exercise Prices	Number Outstanding	Weighted Average Remaining Contractual Life	Weighted Average Exercise Price	Number Exercisable	Weighted Average Exercise Price
$ 3.10 to 5.61	1,271	6.2	$ 5.59	311	$ 5.53
6.33 to 7.59	1,311	7.3	7.37	43	6.90
8.30 to 9.68	3,054	3.8	8.35	2,434	8.32
9.83 to 12.00	966	4.3	10.32	643	10.02
12.17 to 14.05	2,109	9.1	12.34	74	13.16
14.08 to 15.42	1,878	3.7	14.37	1,465	14.32
15.63 to 19.15	388	9.1	15.81	32	17.80
23.48	4,317	3.1	23.48	4,317	23.48
25.83 to 27.21	1,308	2.1	27.20	1,308	27.20
Total	16,602	4.8	$14.94	10,627	$17.71

(B) Restricted Stock and Restricted Stock Units: Under the company's stock incentive plans, shares of restricted stock are granted in the name of an employee or a non-employee director, who has all the rights of a shareholder, subject to certain restrictions and possible forfeitures. Restrictions on the stock awards generally expire two years to five years from the date of grant. The market value, at the grant date, of all restricted shares granted has been recorded as unearned compensation and is a component of stockholders' equity. Unearned compensation is expensed over the restriction periods and included in stock-based compensation expense in the consolidated statements of operations.

Total restricted stock awards of 0.4 million shares of common stock were granted in fiscal 2005. Total restricted stock awards of 2.5 million shares were granted in fiscal 2004. Beginning in fiscal 2004, the company issued performance-based shares, which are considered restricted stock awards. The vesting of these shares is based on the company achieving operating profit margin targets for fiscal 2006. During the fourth quarter of fiscal 2005, management determined that it is unlikely the performance targets related to the performance-based shares issued in fiscal 2004 will be met. Accordingly, the company reversed the compensation expense of $6.5 million recorded to date. As a result of the reversal, compensation expense related to restricted stock was a benefit of $1.6 million in fiscal 2005. Compensation expense related to restricted stock awards was $11.4 million in fiscal 2004 and $20.0 million in fiscal 2003. As of February 28, 2005, 1.9 million restricted shares of common stock were outstanding.

In fiscal 2003, the company began issuing restricted stock units. Restricted stock units are granted in the name of an employee or a non-employee director, who is entitled to receive dividends, but has no voting rights for any restricted stock units held. The restricted stock units are redeemed for company stock once the deferral restriction period has been satisfied. If these restricted stock units are forfeited or cancelled, the shares reserved for the restricted stock units are available for granting. A total of 130,465 restricted stock units was granted in fiscal 2005. A total of 80,464 restricted stock units was granted in fiscal 2004. A total of 474,134 restricted stock units was granted in fiscal 2003. The cost of grants, as determined by the market prices of the common stock at the grant dates, is recognized over the vesting period, generally three years, and is included in stock-based compensation expense on the consolidated statements of operations. Compensation expense related to restricted stock units was $1.4 million in fiscal 2005, $2.0 million in fiscal 2004 and $0.8 million in fiscal 2003.

(C) Employee Stock Purchase Plan: The company has an employee stock purchase plan for all domestic employees meeting certain eligibility criteria. Under the plan, eligible employees may, subject to certain limitations, purchase shares of common stock. The company matches $0.15 for each $1.00 contributed by employees. Purchases are limited to 10 percent of an employee's eligible compensation, up to a maximum of $13,000 per year. The company has authorized 18.5 million shares of common stock for purchase under the plan. Under the plan, certain officers of the company may by written consent increase the maximum number of shares of the company's common stock that may be purchased under the plan as they deem necessary to accommodate cumulative purchases of common stock for any calendar year. However, the officers may not increase the number of shares reserved for issuance under the plan by more than 1% of the number of shares of common stock outstanding as of December 31st of the previous calendar year. If not terminated earlier by the company's board of directors, the plan will terminate at the earlier of (1) the last business day of any month that participating employees become entitled to purchase a number of shares of common stock greater than the number of shares remaining unpurchased out of the total number of shares that may be purchased under the plan, or (2) June 1, 2014. At February 28, 2005, a total of 2.0 million shares remained available under the plan. During fiscal 2005, 0.5 million shares of common stock were issued to or purchased on the open market on behalf of employees. During fiscal 2004, 1.0 million shares of common stock were issued to or purchased on the open market on behalf of employees. During fiscal 2003, 1.2 million shares of common stock were issued to or purchased on the open market on behalf of employees. The average price per share of common stock purchased under the plan was $13.85 in fiscal 2005, $9.31 in fiscal 2004 and $13.32 in fiscal 2003. The company match totaled $0.8 million in fiscal 2005, $1.1 million in fiscal 2004 and $1.6 million in fiscal 2003 and is included in stock-based compensation expense in the consolidated statements of operations.

16. EMPLOYEE BENEFITS PLANS

(A) Pension Plans: The company has a noncontributory defined benefit pension plan covering the majority of domestic segment full-time employees who are at least 21 years of age and have completed one year of service. The cost of the program is being funded currently. Plan benefits generally are based on years of service and average compensation. The company also has an unfunded nonqualified benefit restoration plan that restores retirement benefits for domestic segment senior executives who are affected by Internal Revenue Code limitations on benefits provided under the company's pension plan.

The pension plan was frozen as of February 28, 2005, except for employees who were (i) within three years of their early retirement date or normal retirement date; (ii) had reached their early or normal retirement date; or (iii) were permanently disabled before March 1, 2005. As a result of the pension plan freeze, all affected employees retain any benefits accumulated to the effective date, but are no longer eligible to increase their benefit. The benefit restoration plan was frozen as of February 28, 2005, to provide benefits for participants who, as of that date, were within 10 years of attaining their early retirement date or normal retirement date. The impact of freezing these plans is a curtailment charge of $1.1 million in the fiscal year ended February 28, 2005.

The company uses the last day of its fiscal year as a measurement date for determining pension plan assets and obligations. The change in projected benefit obligation, change in plan assets and reconciliation of funded status for the plans were as follows:

(Amounts in millions)	Years Ended February 28 or 29 2005	2004
Change in projected benefit obligation:		
Projected benefit obligation at beginning of year	$261.9	$203.6
Service cost	14.0	15.9
Interest cost	15.6	13.3
Actuarial loss [(a)]	0.8	36.5
Benefits paid	(6.2)	(6.1)
Curtailments	(43.4)	–
Participant transfers to CarMax	–	(1.3)
Projected benefit obligation at end of year	$242.7	$261.9
Change in plan assets:		
Fair value of plan assets at beginning of year	$194.3	$148.3
Actual return on plan assets	20.3	47.4
Employer contributions	18.5	5.3
Adjustment for CarMax separation	–	(0.6)
Benefits paid	(6.2)	(6.1)
Fair value of plan assets at end of year	$226.9	$194.3
Reconciliation of funded status:		
Funded status	$ (15.8)	$ (67.6)
Unrecognized actuarial loss	26.0	77.4
Unrecognized prior service benefit	1.0	2.7
Net prepaid asset recognized [(b)]	$ 11.2	$ 12.6

(a) Actuarial loss for fiscal 2004 results primarily from the change in the discount rate from 6.60 percent to 6.00 percent.

(b) At February 28, 2005, amount includes an asset for the defined benefit pension plan of $24.3 million, which is included in other assets, and a liability for the benefit restoration plan of $13.1 million, which is included in other liabilities on the consolidated balance sheet. At February 29, 2004, amount includes an asset for the defined benefit pension plan of $23.7 million, which is included in other assets, and a liability for the benefit restoration plan of $11.1 million, which is included in other liabilities on the consolidated balance sheet.

The components of net pension expense for the plans were as follows:

(Amounts in millions)	Years Ended February 28 or 29 2005	2004	2003
Service cost	$14.0	$15.9	$14.9
Interest cost	15.6	13.3	13.4
Expected return on plan assets	(16.4)	(14.5)	(13.4)
Amortization of prior service cost	0.5	0.5	0.3
Recognized actuarial loss	5.0	3.3	0.5
Loss due to curtailment	1.1	–	–
Net pension expense	$19.8	$18.4	$15.7

Benefit obligations are determined using assumptions at the end of each fiscal year and are not impacted by the expected rate of return on plan assets. The weighted average assumptions used in computing the benefit obligations for the plans were as follows:

	Years Ended February 28 or 29 2005	2004
Weighted average discount rate	5.75%	6.00%
Rate of increase in compensation levels	5.00%	5.00%

Net pension expense is determined using assumptions at the beginning of each fiscal year. The weighted average assumptions used in computing net pension expense for the plans were as follows:

	Years Ended February 28 or 29 2005	2004	2003
Weighted average discount rate	6.00%	6.60%	7.25%
Rate of increase in compensation levels	5.00%	5.00%	6.00%
Expected rate of return on plan assets	8.25%	8.25%	9.00%

The percentage composition of assets held by the pension plan was as follows:

	At February 28 or 29 2005	2004
Domestic equity	69%	73%
International equity	18	18
Cash and cash equivalents	10	6
Other	3	3
Total	100%	100%

The plan's overall investment objective is to provide a long-term return that, along with company contributions, is expected to meet future benefit payment requirements. The company engages a third party to advise the company on both asset allocations and individual fund managers. At February 28, 2005, the plan's target asset allocation was 75 percent domestic equity, 20 percent international equity and five percent other. The plan's target allocation is determined by taking into consideration the amounts and timing of projected liabilities, the company's funding policies and expected returns on various asset classes. To develop the expected long-term rate of return on assets, the company considered the historical returns and the future expectations for returns for each asset class, as well as the target asset allocations. Plan assets did not include any shares of the company's common stock at February 28, 2005, or February 29, 2004.

Company contributions to the defined benefit pension plan were $18.0 million in fiscal 2005, $5.0 million in fiscal 2004 and $52.9 million in fiscal 2003. No contributions are required during fiscal 2006 under applicable law for this pension plan. The company intends to make any contributions necessary to meet ERISA minimum funding standards and will make additional contributions as needed to ensure that the fair value of plan assets at February 28, 2006, exceeds the accumulated benefit obligation. The company does not expect to make a contribution in fiscal 2006. The accumulated benefit obligation for the defined benefit pension plan was $220.4 million at February 28, 2005, and $189.1 million at February 29, 2004.

The expected benefit payments of the pension plan for the next 10 fiscal years are as follows:

Fiscal Year	(Amounts in millions)
2006	$ 3.6
2007	$ 3.9
2008	$ 4.4
2009	$ 5.0
2010	$ 5.7
2011 through 2015	$44.5

The accumulated benefit obligation under the benefit restoration plan was $13.6 million at February 28, 2005, and $11.5 million at February 29, 2004. Company contributions to the benefit restoration plan were $463,000 in fiscal 2005, $294,000 in fiscal 2004 and $73,000 in fiscal 2003. A contribution of $618,000, which is equal to the expected benefit payments, is expected to be made to this plan during fiscal 2006.

The expected benefit payments of the benefit restoration plan for the next 10 fiscal years are as follows:

Fiscal Year	(Amounts in thousands)
2006	$ 618
2007	$ 705
2008	$ 771
2009	$ 824
2010	$ 910
2011 through 2015	$5,173

(B) 401(k) Plan and Registered Retirement Savings Plan: The company sponsors a 401(k) plan for domestic segment employees meeting certain eligibility criteria. Under the plan, eligible employees can contribute up to 40 percent of their salaries up to the annual limit as designated by the Internal Revenue Service. Effective January 1, 2005, the company adopted a safe harbor matching formula for the plan. The company matches $1.00 for each $1.00 contributed by an employee on the first three percent of an employee's salary, and $0.50 for each $1.00 on the next two percent of an employee's salary. Prior to January 1, 2005, the company matched $0.25 for each $1.00 contributed by an employee up to five percent of an employee's salary. The company's expense for this plan was $3.6 million in fiscal 2005, $2.7 million in fiscal 2004 and $3.6 million in fiscal 2003 and is included in selling, general and administrative expenses on the consolidated statements of operations.

The company sponsors a group registered retirement savings plan for all international segment employees, under which full-time and qualifying part-time employees with at least 12 months service may join the plan and contribute up to three percent of their salaries. Employee contributions are matched dollar for dollar by the company. Both employee and employer contributions are invested in a broad range of investment options. After membership in the plan for 12 months, an employee may elect to contribute up to an additional two percent of his salary to the plan, which is also matched dollar for dollar by the company. These additional contributions are also invested in a broad range of investment options. The company's expense for this plan was $631,000 in fiscal 2005.

17. DISCONTINUED OPERATIONS

Cash flows related to discontinued operations have been segregated on the consolidated statements of cash flows.

(A) Bankcard Operation: On November 18, 2003, the company completed the sale of its bankcard finance operation to FleetBoston Financial. Bankcard results are presented as results from discontinued operations.

For fiscal 2005, the net loss from the discontinued bankcard operation totaled $1.2 million, which is comprised of post-closing adjustments related to the sale of the bankcard operation. For fiscal 2004, the after-tax loss from the discontinued bankcard operation totaled $90.0 million, compared with after-tax earnings of $25.6 million for fiscal 2003. These results include bankcard-related income generated by a subsidiary that provides reinsurance and indemnification related to credit protection products sold by the finance operation.

(B) CarMax: On September 10, 2002, the company's shareholders approved the separation of the CarMax Group from Circuit City Stores, Inc. and the company's board of directors authorized the redemption of the company's CarMax Group common stock and the distribution of CarMax, Inc. common stock to effect the separation. On October 1, 2002, the separation was effective and CarMax, Inc. became an independent, separately traded public company. Each outstanding share of CarMax Group common stock was redeemed in exchange for one share of CarMax, Inc. common stock. In addition, each holder of Circuit City Group common stock received as a tax-free distribution 0.313879 of a share of CarMax, Inc. common stock for each share of Circuit City Group common stock owned as of September 16, 2002, the record date for the distribution. CarMax results are presented as results from discontinued operations. The company recorded no gain or loss as a result of the separation.

With the separation, CarMax paid a special dividend of $28.4 million to Circuit City Stores, Inc. in recognition of the company's continuing contingent liability on leases related to 23 CarMax locations. At February 28, 2005, the future minimum fixed lease obligations on these 23 leases totaled $422.9 million.

In connection with the separation, the company and CarMax entered into a transition services agreement, under which the company provides CarMax services that currently include administrative services, computer center support and telecommunication services, with initial terms ranging from six to 24 months and varying renewal options. Including a ten percent markup, the company billed CarMax $696,000 during fiscal 2005, $7.0 million during fiscal 2004 and $6.7 million during fiscal 2003 for services provided under the agreement. A tax allocation agreement, which generally provides that pre-separation taxes attributable to the business of each party will be borne solely by that party, also was executed upon the separation.

The discontinued CarMax operations had no impact on the net earnings of the company for fiscal 2005 or fiscal 2004. Net earnings from the discontinued CarMax operations were $62.0 million for fiscal 2003, representing CarMax results for the seven months prior to the separation date.

(C) Divx: On June 16, 1999, Digital Video Express announced that it would cease marketing the Divx home video system and discontinue operations. Divx results are presented as results from discontinued operations. The provision for commitments under licensing agreements was reduced $4.6 million in fiscal 2005, reducing accrued expenses and other current liabilities related to the former Divx operations to zero on the consolidated balance sheet at February 28, 2005. This reduction benefited the fiscal 2005 net earnings from discontinued operations by $3.0 million. The provision for commitments under licensing agreements was reduced $2.3 million in fiscal 2004. This reduction benefited the fiscal 2004 net loss from discontinued operations by $1.5 million. The company has no further commitments related to the Divx operation. The discontinued Divx operations had no impact on the net earnings of the company for fiscal 2003.

18. SEGMENT INFORMATION

The company has two reportable segments: its domestic segment and its international segment. The company identified these segments based on its management reporting structure and the nature of the products and services offered by each segment. The domestic segment is primarily engaged in the business of selling brand-name consumer electronics, personal computers and entertainment software in the United States. The international segment is primarily engaged in the business of selling private-label and brand-name consumer electronics products in Canada. Prior to the second quarter of fiscal 2005, the company had a third reportable segment, its finance operation. The company completed the sale of its private-label finance operation, comprised of its private-label and Visa co-branded credit card programs, to Chase Card Services on May 25, 2004. Results from the private-label finance operation, including transition and transaction costs of approximately $6 million related to the sale of the operation, are included in finance income. See Note 4 for additional discussion of finance income. The company has entered into an arrangement under which Chase Card Services is offering private-label and co-branded credit cards to new and existing customers and providing credit card services to all cardholders. The earnings contribution from that arrangement of $7.8 million for fiscal 2005 is included in net sales and operating revenues on the consolidated statement of operations and is included in the domestic retail segment.

Revenue by reportable segment and the reconciliation to the consolidated statements of operations were as follows:

(Amounts in millions)	Years Ended February 28 or 29 2005	2004	2003
Domestic segment	$10,017.5	$9,857.1	$10,054.9
International segment	454.9	–	–
Finance operation	28.1	120.9	107.3
Total revenues	10,500.5	9,978.0	10,162.2
Less: securitization income*	28.1	120.9	107.3
Net sales and operating revenues	$10,472.4	$9,857.1	$10,054.9

**Securitization income is included in finance income, which reflects the results of the finance operation and is reported separately from net sales and operating revenues on the statements of operations.*

The earnings (loss) from continuing operations before income taxes by reportable segment and the reconciliation to the consolidated statements of operations were as follows:

(Amounts in millions)	Years Ended February 28 or 29 2005	2004	2003
Domestic segment	$57.8	$(33.9)	$(32.8)
International segment	32.4	–	–
Finance operation	5.6	32.7	27.3
Earnings (loss) from continuing operations before income taxes	$95.8	$ (1.2)	$ (5.5)

Prior to the acquisition of InterTAN, the measure of segment profit or loss reviewed by the chief operating decision maker was earnings from continuing operations before income taxes. Subsequent to the acquisition, the measure of segment profit or loss reviewed by the chief operating decision maker is net earnings from continuing operations. Accordingly, the table below presents income tax provision for the domestic and international segment for fiscal 2005.

(Amounts in millions)	2005
Domestic segment	$23.2
International segment	12.7
Income tax provision	$35.9

Total assets by reportable segment and the reconciliation to the consolidated balance sheets were as follows:

(Amounts in millions)	Years Ended February 28 or 29 2005	2004	2003
Domestic segment	$3,354.7	$3,129.2	$3,121.7
International segment	434.7	–	–
Finance operation	–	601.3	423.1
Discontinued operations	–	–	395.8
Total assets	$3,789.4	$3,730.5	$3,940.6

Goodwill and other intangible assets by reportable segment were as follows:

(Amounts in millions)	Years Ended February 28 or 29 2005	2004	2003
Domestic segment	$ 5.3	$ –	$ –
International segment	241.9	–	–
Total goodwill and other intangible assets	$247.2	$ –	$ –

Depreciation and amortization by reportable segment were as follows:

(Amounts in millions)	Years Ended February 28 or 29 2005	2004	2003
Domestic segment	$144.8	$197.6	$159.8
International segment	10.0	–	–
Total depreciation and amortization	$154.8	$197.6	$159.8

Capital expenditures by reportable segment were as follows:

(Amounts in millions)	Years Ended February 28 or 29 2005	2004	2003
Domestic segment	$260.0	$175.8	$150.8
International segment	9.2	–	–
Total capital expenditures	$269.2	$175.8	$150.8

19. SUPPLEMENTAL CONSOLIDATED STATEMENTS OF CASH FLOWS INFORMATION

The following table summarizes supplemental cash flow information.

(Amounts in millions)	Years Ended February 28 2005	2004	2003
Cash paid during the year for:			
Interest	$ 2.5	$ 3.0	$ 1.8
Income taxes	$152.8	$36.3	$107.9
Non-cash investing and financing activities:			
Asset acquired from variable interest entity	$ –	$12.6	$ –
Liability assumed from variable interest entity	$ –	$12.6	$ –
Reduction of liability related to the discontinued Divx operation	$ 4.6	$ 2.3	$ –
Supplemental schedule of non-cash investing and financing activities:			
Capital lease obligation	$ 2.8	$ –	$ –
Acquisition of InterTAN:			
Fair value of assets acquired:			
Cash and cash equivalents	$ 30.6	$ –	$ –
Merchandise inventory	88.8	–	–
Property and equipment, net	42.6	–	–
Goodwill	185.4	–	–
Other intangible assets	28.0	–	–
Other assets	14.1	–	–
Total fair value of assets acquired	389.6	–	–
Less:			
Liabilities assumed	93.2	–	–
Cash acquired	30.6	–	–
Stock options issued	6.5	–	–
Acquisition of InterTAN, net of cash acquired	$259.3	$ –	$ –
Other acquisitions:			
Fair value of assets acquired	$ 13.4	$ –	$ –
Less: liabilities assumed	4.0	–	–
Other acquisitions	$ 9.5	$ –	$ –

20. RECENT ACCOUNTING PRONOUNCEMENTS

In December 2004, the FASB issued SFAS No. 123 (revised 2004), “Share-Based Payment.” SFAS No. 123(R) requires companies to record compensation expense based on the fair value of employee stock-based compensation awards. The statement also requires that the compensation expense be recognized over the period during which the employee is required to provide service in exchange for the award. SFAS No. 123(R) will be effective for the company’s first quarter of fiscal 2007. The company has not yet determined the impact of adopting this standard. See Note 15(A) for information regarding the company’s adoption of SFAS No. 123.

21. QUARTERLY FINANCIAL DATA (UNAUDITED)

(Amounts in millions except per share data)	First Quarter		Second Quarter		Third Quarter		Fourth Quarter		Year	
	2005	2004	2005	2004	2005	2004	2005	2004	2005	2004
Net sales and operating revenues	$2,094.4	$1,955.5	$2,376.5	$2,178.5	$2,532.4	$2,427.8	$3,469.1	$3,295.2	$10,472.4	$9,857.1
Gross profit	$ 494.7	$ 459.1	$ 591.2	$ 498.2	$ 637.8	$ 543.6	$ 845.0	$ 783.2	$ 2,568.7	$2,284.0
Net (loss) earnings from:										
Continuing operations	$ (5.2)	$ (28.1)	$ (11.4)	$ (39.3)	$ (5.9)	$ (28.1)	$ 82.5	$ 94.7	$ 60.0	$ (0.8)
Discontinued operations	(0.7)	(18.6)	(0.5)	(90.3)	–	25.5	3.0	(5.1)	1.7	(88.5)
Net (loss) earnings	$ (5.9)	$ (46.7)	$ (11.9)	$ (129.6)	$ (5.9)	$ (2.5)	$ 85.4	$ 89.6	$ 61.7	$ (89.3)
Net (loss) earnings per share:										
Basic:										
Continuing operations	$ (0.03)	$ (0.14)	$ (0.06)	$ (0.19)	$ (0.03)	$ (0.14)	$ 0.44	$ 0.46	$ 0.31	$ –
Discontinued operations	–	(0.09)	–	(0.44)	–	0.12	0.02	(0.02)	0.01	(0.43)
	$ (0.03)	$ (0.23)	$ (0.06)	$ (0.63)	$ (0.03)	$ (0.01)	$ 0.45	$ 0.44	$ 0.32	$ (0.43)
Diluted:										
Continuing operations	$ (0.03)	$ (0.14)	$ (0.06)	$ (0.19)	$ (0.03)	$ (0.14)	$ 0.43	$ 0.46	$ 0.31	$ –
Discontinued operations	–	(0.09)	–	(0.44)	–	0.12	0.02	(0.02)	0.01	(0.43)
	$ (0.03)	$ (0.23)	$ (0.06)	$ (0.63)	$ (0.03)	$ (0.01)	$ 0.45	$ 0.43	$ 0.31	$ (0.43)

Consolidated results include results from InterTAN from the acquisition date, May 12, 2004. Results for fiscal 2005 include an after tax charge of $4.2 million for the cumulative impact of a revision to the company's lease accounting practices during the fourth quarter of fiscal 2005. Consolidated results also reflect the reclassification of revenues, costs and expenses relating primarily to mobile audio installations for the domestic segment.

Year-to-date earnings per share are calculated by dividing year-to-date earnings by the weighted average shares outstanding for the full year. Therefore, year-to-date earnings per share do not equal the sum of the quarterly earnings per share.

Report of Independent Registered Public Accounting Firm

The Board of Directors and Stockholders
Circuit City Stores, Inc.:

We have audited the accompanying consolidated balance sheets of Circuit City Stores, Inc. and subsidiaries (the Company) as of February 28, 2005 and February 29, 2004, and the related consolidated statements of operations, stockholders' equity and comprehensive income, and cash flows for each of the fiscal years in the three-year period ended February 28, 2005. These consolidated financial statements are the responsibility of the Company's management. Our responsibility is to express an opinion on these consolidated financial statements based on our audits.

We conducted our audits in accordance with the standards of the Public Company Accounting Oversight Board (United States). Those standards require that we plan and perform the audit to obtain reasonable assurance about whether the financial statements are free of material misstatement. An audit includes examining, on a test basis, evidence supporting the amounts and disclosures in the financial statements. An audit also includes assessing the accounting principles used and significant estimates made by management, as well as evaluating the overall financial statement presentation. We believe that our audits provide a reasonable basis for our opinion.

In our opinion, the consolidated financial statements referred to above present fairly, in all material respects, the financial position of Circuit City Stores, Inc. and subsidiaries as of February 28, 2005 and February 29, 2004, and the results of their operations and their cash flows for each of the fiscal years in the three-year period ended February 28, 2005, in conformity with U.S. generally accepted accounting principles.

We also have audited, in accordance with the standards of the Public Company Accounting Oversight Board (United States), the effectiveness of Circuit City Stores, Inc.'s internal control over financial reporting as of February 28, 2005, based on criteria established in *Internal Control-Integrated Framework* issued by the Committee of Sponsoring Organizations of the Treadway Commission (COSO), and our report dated May 6, 2005 expressed an unqualified opinion on management's assessment of, and the effective operation of, internal control over financial reporting.

/S/ KPMG LLP

Richmond, Virginia
May 6, 2005

Report of Independent Registered Public Accounting Firm

The Board of Directors and Stockholders
Circuit City Stores, Inc.:

We have audited management's assessment, included in the accompanying Management's Report on Internal Control over Financial Reporting, that Circuit City Stores, Inc. (the Company) maintained effective internal control over financial reporting as of February 28, 2005, based on criteria established in *Internal Control—Integrated Framework* issued by the Committee of Sponsoring Organizations of the Treadway Commission (COSO). The Company's management is responsible for maintaining effective internal control over financial reporting and for its assessment of the effectiveness of internal control over financial reporting. Our responsibility is to express an opinion on management's assessment and an opinion on the effectiveness of the Company's internal control over financial reporting based on our audit.

We conducted our audit in accordance with the standards of the Public Company Accounting Oversight Board (United States). Those standards require that we plan and perform the audit to obtain reasonable assurance about whether effective internal control over financial reporting was maintained in all material respects. Our audit included obtaining an understanding of internal control over financial reporting, evaluating management's assessment, testing and evaluating the design and operating effectiveness of internal control, and performing such other procedures as we considered necessary in the circumstances. We believe that our audit provides a reasonable basis for our opinion.

A company's internal control over financial reporting is a process designed to provide reasonable assurance regarding the reliability of financial reporting and the preparation of financial statements for external purposes in accordance with generally accepted accounting principles. A company's internal control over financial reporting includes those policies and procedures that (1) pertain to the maintenance of records that, in reasonable detail, accurately and fairly reflect the transactions and dispositions of the assets of the Company; (2) provide reasonable assurance that transactions are recorded as necessary to permit preparation of financial statements in accordance with generally accepted accounting principles, and that receipts and expenditures of the Company are being made only in accordance with authorizations of management and directors of the Company; and (3) provide reasonable assurance regarding prevention or timely detection of unauthorized acquisition, use, or disposition of the Company's assets that could have a material effect on the financial statements.

Because of its inherent limitations, internal control over financial reporting may not prevent or detect misstatements. Also, projections of any evaluation of effectiveness to future periods are subject to the risk that controls may become inadequate because of changes in conditions, or that the degree of compliance with the policies or procedures may deteriorate.

In our opinion, management's assessment that the Company maintained effective internal control over financial reporting as of February 28, 2005, is fairly stated, in all material respects, based on criteria established in *Internal Control—Integrated Framework* issued by the Committee of Sponsoring Organizations of the Treadway Commission (COSO). Also, in our opinion, the Company maintained, in all material respects, effective internal control over financial reporting as of February 28, 2005, based on criteria established in *Internal Control—Integrated Framework* issued by COSO.

In conducting its evaluation of the effectiveness of internal control over financial reporting, the Company did not include the internal controls of InterTAN, Inc., which the Company acquired on May 12, 2004. The acquired entity constituted approximately 11 percent of the consolidated assets of the Company as of February 28, 2005, and approximately 4 percent of consolidated revenues and 33 percent of consolidated net earnings from continuing operations of the Company for the year then ended. Refer to Note 3 of the consolidated financial statements for a further discussion of the acquisition and its impact on the Company's consolidated financial statements. Our audit of internal control over financial reporting of the Company also excluded an evaluation of the internal control over financial reporting of InterTAN, Inc.

We also have audited, in accordance with the standards of the Public Company Accounting Oversight Board (United States), the consolidated balance sheets of Circuit City Stores, Inc. and subsidiaries as of February 28, 2005 and February 29, 2004, and the related consolidated statements of operations, stockholders' equity and comprehensive income, and cash flows for each of the fiscal years in the three-year period ended February 28, 2005, and our report dated May 6, 2005 expressed an unqualified opinion on those consolidated financial statements.

/s/KPMG LLP

Richmond, Virginia
May 6, 2005

Item 9. Changes in and Disagreements with Accountants on Accounting and Financial Disclosure.

None.

Item 9A. Controls and Procedures.

Evaluation of Disclosure Controls and Procedures

Under the supervision and with the participation of the company's management, including the chief executive officer and chief financial officer, the company has evaluated the effectiveness of its "disclosure controls and procedures," as that term is defined in Rule 13a-15(e) of the Securities Exchange Act of 1934, as amended, as of the end of the period covered by this Annual Report on Form 10-K. Based upon their evaluation, the chief executive officer and chief financial officer concluded that the company's disclosure controls and procedures are effective.

Management's Report on Internal Control over Financial Reporting

Our management is responsible for establishing and maintaining adequate internal control over financial reporting, as such term is defined in Exchange Act Rule 13a-15(f) under the Securities Exchange Act of 1934, as amended. Under the supervision and with the participation of management, including our principal executive officer and principal financial officer, an evaluation of the effectiveness of internal control over financial reporting was conducted based on the framework in *Internal Control - Integrated Framework* issued by the Committee of Sponsoring Organizations of the Treadway Commission (COSO).

In conducting our evaluation of the effectiveness of the internal control over financial reporting, we did not include the internal controls of InterTAN, Inc., which the company acquired on May 12, 2004. The acquired entity constituted approximately 11 percent of the consolidated assets of the company as of February 28, 2005, and approximately 4 percent of consolidated revenues and 33 percent of consolidated net earnings from continuing operations of the company for the year then ended. Refer to Note 3 of the consolidated financial statements for a further discussion of the acquisition and its impact on our consolidated financial statements.

Based on our evaluation under the framework in *Internal Control - Integrated Framework*, our management concluded that internal control over financial reporting was effective as of February 28, 2005.

Our management's assessment of the effectiveness of internal control over financial reporting as of February 28, 2005, has been audited by KPMG LLP, an independent registered public accounting firm, as stated in its report, which is included in this Annual Report on Form 10-K.

Changes in Control over Financial Reporting

There were no changes in the company's internal control over financial reporting in the quarter ended February 28, 2005, that have materially affected, or are reasonably likely to materially affect, the company's internal control over financial reporting.

Item 9B. Other Information.

None.

PART III

With the exception of the information incorporated by reference from the company's Proxy Statement in Items 10, 11, 12 and 14 of Part III of this Annual Report on Form 10-K, the company's Proxy Statement dated May 13, 2005, is not to be deemed filed as a part of this Report.

Item 10. Directors and Executive Officers of the Company.

The information appearing under the heading "Item One – Election of Directors" on pages 3 through 5 of the company's Proxy Statement dated May 13, 2005, is incorporated in this item by reference.

The information appearing under the heading "Information Concerning the Board of Directors and Its Committees" on pages 6 through 8 of the company's Proxy Statement dated May 13, 2005, is incorporated in this item by reference.

The information appearing under the heading "Section 16(a) Beneficial Ownership Reporting Compliance" on page 18 of the company's Proxy Statement dated May 13, 2005, is incorporated in this item by reference.

The company's code of business conduct is available on the company's investor information homepage at http://investor.circuitcity.com.

Information concerning the company's executive officers is included in Part I of this report under the caption "Executive Officers of the Company."

Item 11. Executive Compensation.

The information appearing under the heading "Compensation of Executive Officers" on pages 9 through 15 of the company's Proxy Statement dated May 13, 2005, is incorporated in this item by reference.

The information appearing under the heading "Employment Agreements and Change-in-Control Arrangements" on pages 14 and 15 of the company's Proxy Statement dated May 13, 2005, is incorporated in this item by reference.

The information appearing under the heading "Compensation of Directors" on pages 8 and 9 of the company's Proxy Statement dated May 13, 2005, is incorporated in this item by reference.

Item 12. Security Ownership of Certain Beneficial Owners and Management and Related Shareholder Matters.

The information appearing under the heading "Beneficial Ownership of Securities" on pages 16 and 17 of the company's Proxy Statement dated May 13, 2005, is incorporated in this item by reference.

The information appearing under the heading "Equity Compensation Plans Information" on pages 13 and 14 of the company's Proxy Statement dated May 13, 2005, is incorporated in this item by reference.

Item 13. Certain Relationships and Related Transactions.

None.

Item 14. Principal Accounting Fees and Services.

The information appearing under the heading "Item Four – Ratification of Appointment of Independent Registered Public Accounting Firm" on page 32 of the company's Proxy Statement dated May 13, 2005, is incorporated in this item by reference.

PART IV

Item 15. Exhibits, Financial Statement Schedules

(a) The following are filed as a part of this report.

1. Financial Statements. All financial statements as set forth under Item 8 of this report.
2. Financial Statement Schedules. The following financial statement schedules of Circuit City Stores, Inc. for the fiscal years ended February 28, 2005, February 29, 2004, and February 28, 2003, are filed as part of this report and should be read in conjunction with the consolidated financial statements of Circuit City Stores, Inc. and the notes thereto, described in Item 15(a)1.

   Schedule II Valuation and Qualifying Accounts and Reserves — S-1

   Report of Independent Registered Public Accounting Firm on Financial Statement Schedule — S-2

   Schedules not listed above have been omitted because they are not applicable or are not required or the information required to be set forth therein is included in the consolidated financial statements or notes thereto.
3. Exhibits. The exhibits listed on the accompanying Exhibit Index immediately following the financial schedules are filed as part of, or are incorporated by reference into, this report.

SIGNATURES

Pursuant to the requirements of Section 13 or 15(d) of the Securities Exchange Act of 1934, the Registrant has duly caused this report to be signed on its behalf by the undersigned, thereunto duly authorized.

CIRCUIT CITY STORES, INC.

May 13, 2005 By: /s/W. Alan McCollough
W. Alan McCollough
Chairman of the Board and Chief Executive Officer

Pursuant to the requirements of the Securities Exchange Act of 1934, this report has been signed by the following persons on behalf of the Registrant and in the capacities indicated on May 13, 2005:

Signature	Title
/s/W. Alan McCollough W. Alan McCollough	Chairman of the Board and Chief Executive Officer (Principal Executive Officer)
/s/Michael E. Foss Michael E. Foss	Executive Vice President and Chief Financial Officer (Principal Financial Officer)
/s/Philip J. Dunn Philip J. Dunn	Senior Vice President, Treasurer, Controller and Chief Accounting Officer (Principal Accounting Officer)
Ronald M. Brill* Ronald M. Brill	Director
Carolyn H. Byrd* Carolyn H. Byrd	Director
Barbara S. Feigin* Barbara S. Feigin	Director
E.V. Goings * E.V. Goings	Director
James F. Hardymon* James F. Hardymon	Director
Alan Kane* Alan Kane	Director
Allen B. King* Allen B. King	Director
Mikael Salovaara* Mikael Salovaara	Director
J. Patrick Spainhour* J. Patrick Spainhour	Director
Carolyn Y. Woo* Carolyn Y. Woo	Director

*By: /s/W. Alan McCollough
W. Alan McCollough,
Attorney-In-Fact

Schedule II

Valuation and Qualifying Accounts and Reserves
(Amounts in thousands)

Description	Balance at Beginning of Year	Charged to Income	Charge-offs less Recoveries	Balance at End of Year
Year ended February 28, 2003:				
Allowance for doubtful accounts	$ 660	$ 4,790	$ (4,375)	$ 1,075
Year ended February 29, 2004:				
Allowance for doubtful accounts	$ 1,075	$ 3,049	$ (3,577)	$ 547
Year ended February 28, 2005:				
Allowance for doubtful accounts	$ 547	$ 2,420	$ (2,847)	$ 120

Report of Independent Registered Public Accounting Firm

The Board of Directors and Stockholders
Circuit City Stores, Inc.:

Under date of May 6, 2005, we reported on the consolidated balance sheets of Circuit City Stores, Inc. and subsidiaries (the Company) as of February 28, 2005 and February 29, 2004, and the related consolidated statements of operations, stockholders' equity and comprehensive income, and cash flows for each of the fiscal years in the three-year period ended February 28, 2005, as contained in the 2005 annual report to shareholders. In connection with our audits of the aforementioned consolidated financial statements, we also audited the related consolidated financial statement schedule as listed in Item 15(a)2 of this Form 10-K. This financial statement schedule is the responsibility of the Company's management. Our responsibility is to express an opinion on this financial statement schedule based on our audits.

In our opinion, such financial statement schedule, when considered in relation to the basic consolidated financial statements taken as a whole, presents fairly, in all material aspects, the information set forth therein.

/s/KPMG LLP

Richmond, Virginia
May 6, 2005

EXHIBIT INDEX

Articles of Incorporation and Bylaws

3.1 Circuit City Stores, Inc. Amended and Restated Articles of Incorporation, effective February 3, 1997, as amended through October 1, 2002, filed as Exhibit 3(i) to the company's Quarterly Report on Form 10-Q for the quarter ended November 30, 2002 (File No. 1-5767), are expressly incorporated herein by this reference.

3.2 Circuit City Stores, Inc. Bylaws, as amended and restated April 19, 2005, filed as Exhibit 3.1 to the Company's Current Report on Form 8-K filed April 21, 2005 (File No. 1-5767), are expressly incorporated herein by this reference.

Material Contracts

10.1 Circuit City Stores, Inc. 2000 Non-Employee Directors Stock Incentive Plan, as Amended and Restated, Effective August 17, 2004, filed as Exhibit 10.5 to the company's Quarterly Report on Form 10-Q for the quarter ended August 31, 2004 (File No. 1-5767), is expressly incorporated herein by this reference. *

10.2 Circuit City Stores, Inc. Amended and Restated 1989 Non-Employee Directors Stock Option Plan, filed as Exhibit A to the company's Definitive Proxy Statement dated May 9, 1997, for the Annual Meeting of Shareholders held on June 17, 1997 (File No. 1-5767), is expressly incorporated herein by this reference. *

10.3 Amendments adopted June 17, 1997, to the Circuit City Stores, Inc. Amended and Restated 1989 Non-Employee Directors Stock Option Plan filed as Exhibit 10(ii) to the Circuit City Stores, Inc. Quarterly Report on Form 10-Q for the quarter ended May 31, 1997 (File No. 1-5767), are expressly incorporated herein by this reference. *

10.4 Circuit City Stores, Inc. 1994 Stock Incentive Plan, as amended as of January 24, 1997, filed as Annex III to the company's Definitive Proxy Statement dated December 24, 1996, for a Special Meeting of Shareholders held on January 24, 1997 (File No. 1-5767), is expressly incorporated herein by this reference. *

10.5 Amendments effective June 13, 2000, to the Circuit City Stores, Inc. 1994 Stock Incentive Plan as amended, filed as Exhibit 10 to the company's Quarterly Report on form 10-Q for the quarter ended May 31, 2000 (File No. 1-5767), are expressly incorporated herein by this reference. *

10.6 Amendment effective June 15, 1999, to the Circuit City Stores, Inc. 1994 Stock Incentive Plan, as amended, filed as Exhibit 10 to the company's Quarterly Report on Form 10-Q for the quarter ended May 31, 1999 (File No. 1-5767), is expressly incorporated herein by this reference. *

10.7 Circuit City Stores, Inc. 2003 Stock Incentive Plan, as Amended and Restated, Effective August 17, 2004, filed as Exhibit 10.2 to the company's Quarterly Report on Form 10-Q for the quarter ended August 31, 2004 (File No. 1-5767), is expressly incorporated herein by this reference. *

10.8 InterTAN, Inc. Amended and Restated 1996 Stock Option Plan, filed as Exhibit 10.3 to the company's Quarterly Report on Form 10-Q for the quarter ended August 31, 2004 (File No. 1-5767), is expressly incorporated herein by this reference.*

10.9 Form of Non-Qualified Stock Option Grant Letter, filed as exhibit 10.2 to the company's Current Report on Form 8-K filed October 4, 2004 (File No. 1-5767), is expressly incorporated herein by this reference.*

10.10 Form of Restricted Stock Grant Letter, filed as exhibit 10.3 to the company's Current Report on Form 8-K filed October 4, 2004 (File No. 1-5767), is expressly incorporated herein by this reference.*

10.11 Form of Performance Restricted Stock Grant Letter, filed as exhibit 10.4 to the company's Current Report on Form 8-K filed October 4, 2004 (File No. 1-5767), is expressly incorporated herein by this reference.*

10.12 Employment agreement between the company and W. Alan McCollough effective November 19, 2003, filed as Exhibit 10.2 to the company's Quarterly Report on Form 10-Q for the quarter ended November 30, 2003 (File No. 1-5767), is expressly incorporated herein by this reference. *

10.13 Employment agreement between the company and Philip J. Schoonover effective October 4, 2004, filed as Exhibit 10.1 to the company's Current Report on Form 8-K filed October 4, 2004 (File 1-5767), is expressly incorporated herein by this reference. *

10.14 Form of employment agreement between the company and certain executive officers effective June 30, 2003, filed as Exhibit 10.2 to the company's Quarterly Report on Form 10-Q for the quarter ended August 31, 2003 (File No. 1-5767), is expressly incorporated herein by this reference. *

10.15 Severance Agreement and General Release between the Company and John W. Froman effective March 1, 2005, filed as Exhibit 10.1 to the company's Current Report on Form 8-K filed March 2, 2005 (File 1-5767), is expressly incorporated herein by this reference. *

10.16 Employment agreement between the company and Brian E. Levy effective March 30, 2004, filed as Exhibit 10.1 to the company's Quarterly Report on Form 10-Q for the quarter ended May 31, 2004 (File No. 1-5767), is expressly incorporated herein by this reference.*

10.17 Employment agreement between the company and Michael E. Foss effective February 6, 2004, filed herewith.*

10.18 Circuit City Stores, Inc. 2003 Annual Performance-Based Bonus Plan, filed as Appendix C to the company's Definitive Proxy Statement dated May 9, 2003, for an Annual Meeting of Shareholders held on June 17, 2003 (File No. 1-5767), is expressly incorporated herein by this reference. *

10.19 Circuit City Stores, Inc. Restricted Stock Unit Deferral Program under the Circuit City Stores, Inc. 2000 Non-Employee Directors Stock Incentive Plan, filed as Exhibit 10.6 to the company's Quarterly Report on Form 10-Q for the quarter ended August 31, 2004 (File No. 1-5767), is expressly incorporated herein by this reference. *

10.20 Circuit City Stores, Inc. Non-Employee Directors Deferred Compensation Plan, filed as Exhibit 10 to the company's Quarterly Report on Form 10-Q for the quarter ended August 31, 2000 (File No. 1-5767), is expressly incorporated herein by this reference. *

10.21 Program for deferral of director compensation implemented October 1995 filed as Exhibit 10(i) to the company's Quarterly Report on Form 10-Q for the quarter ended November 30, 1995 (File No. 1-5767), is expressly incorporated herein by this reference. *

10.22 Circuit City Stores, Inc. Benefit Restoration Plan, As Amended and Restated Effective February 28, 2005, filed as Exhibit 10.1 to the company's Current Report on Form 8-K filed October 29, 2004 (File 1-5767), is expressly incorporated herein by this reference. *

10.23 Circuit City Stores, Inc. Supplemental 401(k) Plan, Effective March 1, 2005, filed as Exhibit 10.2 to the company's Current Report on Form 8-K filed October 29, 2004 (File 1-5767), is expressly incorporated herein by this reference. *

10.24 The 1984 Circuit City Stores, Inc. Employee Stock Purchase Plan as Amended and Restated Effective August 17, 2004, filed as Exhibit 10.4 to the company's Quarterly Report on Form 10-Q for the quarter ended August 31, 2004 (File No. 1-5767), is expressly incorporated herein by this reference. *

10.25 Amended and Restated Credit Agreement dated as of July 8, 2004, filed as Exhibit 10.1 to the company's Quarterly Report on Form 10-Q for the quarter ended August 31, 2004 (File No. 1-5767), is expressly incorporated herein by this reference.

10.26 First Amendment to Amended and Restated Credit Agreement dated as of November 17, 2004, filed as Exhibit 10.4 to the company's Quarterly Report on Form 10-Q for the quarter ended November 30, 2004 (File No. 1-5767), is expressly incorporated herein by this reference.

10.27 The Consumer Credit Card Program Agreement dated as of January 16, 2004, between Circuit City Stores, Inc and Bank One, Delaware, N.A., filed as Exhibit 10(r) to the company's Annual Report on Form 10-K for the fiscal year ended February 29, 2004 (File No. 1-5767), is expressly incorporated herein by this reference.

10.28 Amendment to Program Agreement, dated as of May 25, 2004, between Circuit City Stores, Inc. and Bank One, Delaware, N.A., filed as Exhibit 10.7 to the company's Quarterly Report on Form 10-Q for the quarter ended August 31, 2004 (File No. 1-5767), is expressly incorporated herein by this reference.

10.29 Amendment #2 to Program Agreement, effective as of May 25, 2004, between Circuit City Stores, Inc. and Bank One, Delaware, N.A., filed as Exhibit 10.8 to the company's Quarterly Report on Form 10-Q for the quarter ended August 31, 2004 (File No. 1-5767), is expressly incorporated herein by this reference.

10.30 Schedule of Non-Employee Director Compensation 2005-2006, filed as Exhibit 10.1 to the company's Current Report on Form 8-K filed April 21, 2005 (File No. 1-5767), is expressly incorporated herein by this reference.*

10.31 Schedule of Compensation for Named Executive Officers, filed herewith.*

10.32 Circuit City Stores, Inc. Executive Deferred Compensation Plan, as Amended and Restated, Effective December 31, 2004, filed as Exhibit 10.3 to the company's Quarterly Report on Form 10-Q for the quarter ended November 30, 2004 (Filed No. 1-5767), is expressly incorporated herein by this reference.*

21.1 Subsidiaries of the Company

23.1 Consent of Independent Registered Public Accounting Firm

24.1 Powers of Attorney

Rule 13a-14(a)/15d-14(a) Certifications

31.1 Certification of CEO under Rule 13a-14(a) of the Securities Exchange Act of 1934

31.2 Certification of CFO under Rule 13a-14(a) of the Securities Exchange Act of 1934

Section 1350 Certifications

32.1 Certification of CEO under Section 906 of the Sarbanes-Oxley Act of 2002

32.2 Certification of CFO under Section 906 of the Sarbanes-Oxley Act of 2002

*Indicates management contracts, compensatory plans or arrangements of the company required to be filed as an exhibit.

BOARD OF DIRECTORS

W. ALAN MCCOLLOUGH
Chairman and Chief Executive Officer

JAMES F. HARDYMON[2,3]
Lead Director; Retired, Chairman and Chief Executive Officer, Textron Inc., a global multi-industry company; Providence, Rhode Island

RONALD M. BRILL[1]
Private Investor; Retired, Executive Vice President and Chief Administrative Officer, The Home Depot Inc., a home improvement retailer; Atlanta, Georgia

CAROLYN H. BYRD[1]
Chairman and Chief Executive Officer, GlobalTech Financial, LLC, a financial services company; Atlanta, Georgia

BARBARA S. FEIGIN[1]
Consultant; Retired, Executive Vice President, Worldwide Director of Strategic Services, Grey Advertising, Inc., a global advertising agency; New York, New York

E.V. GOINGS[2,3]
Chairman and Chief Executive Officer, Tupperware Corporation, a direct seller; Orlando, Florida

ALAN KANE[2,3]
Professor of Retailing, Columbia University Graduate School of Business, Columbia University; New York, New York

ALLEN B. KING[1]
President and Chief Executive Officer, Universal Corporation, a diversified company with operations in tobacco, lumber distribution and agri-products; Richmond, Virginia

MIKAEL SALOVAARA[2,3]
Private Investor; Retired, Partner, Greycliff Partners, a merchant banking firm; Morristown, New Jersey

J. PATRICK SPAINHOUR[1]
Chairman and Chief Executive Officer, Ann Taylor Stores Corporation, a specialty apparel retailer; New York, New York

CAROLYN Y. WOO[2,3]
Dean, Mendoza College of Business, University of Notre Dame; Notre Dame, Indiana

(1) Audit Committee member
(2) Compensation and Personnel Committee member
(3) Nominating and Governance Committee Member

EXECUTIVE OFFICERS

W. ALAN MCCOLLOUGH
Chairman and Chief Executive Officer

PHILIP J. SCHOONOVER
President

MICHAEL E. FOSS
Executive Vice President
Chief Financial Officer

BRIAN E. LEVY
President and Chief Executive Officer, InterTAN

GEORGE D. CLARK, JR.
Senior Vice President
President, Circuit City – Retail Stores

RONALD G. CUTHBERTSON
Senior Vice President
Supply Chain and Inventory Management

WILLIAM C. DENNEY
Senior Vice President
General Merchandise Manager

FIONA P. DIAS
Senior Vice President
President Circuit City Direct

PHILIP J. DUNN
Senior Vice President
Treasurer and Controller

ERIC A. JONAS, JR.
Senior Vice President
Human Resources

MICHAEL L. JONES
Senior Vice President
Chief Information Officer

GARY M. MIERENFELD
Senior Vice President
Store Development, Procurement, Distribution and Service

DOUGLAS T. MOORE
Senior Vice President
Chief Merchandising Officer

MARC J. SIEGER
Senior Vice President
General Merchandise Manager

ERNEST V. SPERANZA
Senior Vice President
Chief Marketing Officer

RANDALL W. WICK
Senior Vice President
General Merchandise Manager

SHAREHOLDER INFORMATION

CORPORATE OFFICES
Circuit City Stores, Inc.
9950 Mayland Drive
Richmond, Virginia 23233-1464

ANNUAL MEETING
June 21, 2005, 10:00 a.m.
The Jepson Alumni Center
The University of Richmond
Richmond, Virginia

STOCK INFORMATION
Listed on the New York Stock Exchange
Circuit City NYSE symbol: CC
There were approximately 6,544 shareholders of record at February 28, 2005.

INDEPENDENT REGISTERED PUBLIC ACCOUNTING FIRM
KPMG LLP
Richmond, Virginia

TRANSFER AGENT AND REGISTRAR
Wells Fargo Bank Minnesota, N.A.
South St. Paul, Minnesota
(800) 401-1957
http://www.wellsfargo.com/com/shareowner_services

RIGHTS AGENT
Wells Fargo Bank Minnesota, N.A.
South St. Paul, Minnesota

SHAREHOLDER INQUIRIES
Office of Investor Relations
(804) 527-4038 or (804) 527-4033

SECURITIES ANALYST INQUIRIES
Bill Cimino
Director of Corporate Communications
(804) 418-8163

WEB SITE
www.circuitcity.com

INVESTOR INFORMATION WEB SITE
http://investor.circuitcity.com